HIDDEN HISTORY *of* UPTOWN & EDGEWATER

HIDDEN HISTORY *of* UPTOWN & EDGEWATER

Patrick Butler

Published by The History Press
Charleston, SC 29403
www.historypress.net

Unless otherwise indicated, all cover and internal photos are courtesy of the Edgewater Historical Society.

First published 2013

Manufactured in the United States

ISBN 978.1.62619.143.3

Library of Congress CIP data applied for.

To my daughter, Kathleen Butler Greenan; my son-in-law, Ryan Greenan; and my two grandsons, Paddy and Declan.

Contents

ACKNOWLEDGEMENTS

Many thanks to:
Kathy Hills, as always, for her continuing help and support.
The Edgewater Historical Society, especially its president, Robert Remer, historian LeRoy Blommaert and archivist Tom Walsh.
Former Sulzer Regional Library director Leah Steele for her guidance and encouragement.

Introduction

If there's any place in Chicago that's been all things to all men, it has to be Edgewater and Uptown.

During Prohibition, it was a hangout for gangsters like Al Capone, who used to chill with Hollywood celebrities at the Green Mill, which reportedly had a secret tunnel for moving booze to the Aragon Ballroom a few blocks east. And the fabled Edgewater Beach Hotel played host to everyone from Babe Ruth and Mahatma Gandhi to FDR, Ike and King Saud.

It's been the erstwhile home of the notorious Lincoln Towing Company, subject of the late Steve Goodman's 1972 folk song "Lincoln Park Pirates" and where entertainer Danny Thomas made a vow that set him on a path of lifelong philanthropy while working at an Edgewater nightclub. Here, too, Deputy Soviet Premier Anastas Mikoyan took a break from the Cold War by stopping to break bread with an ordinary Uptown family, while in Edgewater, a "Kitchen Revolt" by some not-very-ordinary housewives sent once-invulnerable machine ward boss Marty Tuchow on his way to Club Fed.

Edgewater was also where William Heirens dismembered little Suzanne Degnan and home to the "Burglar Cops" moonlighting out of the old Summerdale police station, triggering a seismic scandal that brought in outsider Orlando Wilson, a California criminology professor with little practical police experience.

Now a resurgent entertainment destination whose attractions still include the Green Mill and the Aragon, Uptown's earliest draw was probably

Left: A postcard from the Edgewater Beach Hotel, a home away from home to celebrities ranging from FDR and Mahatma Gandhi to sports luminaries and mob figures.

Below: The Gengler Brothers Saloon at Clark and Summerdale in 1902.

Graceland Cemetery, where German and Swedish immigrants held Sunday picnics and church outings.

In the 1920s, developers bent on equating the rising community with New York got the area officially christened Uptown and named its main drag Broadway. Depression and World War II–era workers shopped at Goldblatt's at Broadway and Leland and partied at the Green Mill, the Aragon and the

Bell ringers lead a 1994 Andersonville parade, recalling a longtime tradition when a bell reminded shopkeepers along Clark Street to sweep their sidewalks.

posh Edgewater Beach Hotel, where big name bands led by legends like Xavier Cugat did live, nationally broadcast radio shows.

But things started going downhill fast by the 1950s. During World War II's housing shortage, luxury apartments around Winthrop and Kenmore between Montrose and Argyle became housing for defense workers, the families of servicemen stationed at Fort Sheridan and the Great Lakes Naval Training Center on the North Shore.

The postwar years saw an influx of Japanese Americans released from internment camps on the condition that they leave the West Coast. A few years later came the flood of unemployed Appalachian whites leaving played-out coal mines in search of increasingly scarce factory work.

By the late 1960s, as mental hospitals closed, thousands of patients were released into "halfway houses" in low-income neighborhoods with little political clout. Before long, Uptown reportedly had more mental health facilities and social service agencies than any other community in Chicago—and possibly the entire country.

Future "Chicago Seven" defendant Rennie Davis co-founded JOIN (Jobs and Income Now), which made some waves but wasn't nearly as successful as Tennessee transplants Chuck Geary and Iberus Hacker, who fought in their own ways to slow the tide of gentrification coming their way in the early 1970s.

Edgewater fared better in the long run. While its Kenmore and Sheridan Road corridors went from upscale to seriously overcrowded by the 1960s with transients, the mentally ill and the indigent elderly, groups like the Edgewater Community Council worked with the Organization of the Northeast to get a moratorium on any new residential after-care facilities—the then-popular euphemism for halfway houses—and even got Edgewater officially separated from Uptown as Chicago's seventy-seventh officially recognized community area.

At the same time, neighborhoods within Edgewater and Uptown were forging their own identities, with Argyle Street becoming "Chinatown North" or "Little Saigon," depending on your point of view, and part of Clark Street becoming a new "Boys' Town," second only to the thriving gay enclave along Lake View's rainbow-colonnaded Halsted Street.

And by all indications, the transformation of Edgewater and Uptown is only beginning.

Uptown

Uptown, Not Hollywood, Was Once the Hub of American Filmdom

Ignored for years, the old Essanay studio building at 1333–45 West Argyle is now part of St. Augustine College, a one-time affiliate of the Chicago Episcopal Diocese that focuses on nontraditional higher education for minority students of all ages.

And probably nothing could be more nontraditional than teaching the cinema arts in the same studio (now the Charlie Chaplin Auditorium) where Gloria Swanson married Wallace Beery and the "Little Tramp" did many of the scenes for *His New Job*. While the once-major studio is long gone, you'll still find two vaults in the basement with warnings and instructions on the safe handling of the highly flammable nitrate-based films used during silent films' infancy.

From 1908 to 1917, the Essanay—founded by George Spoor and William "Broncho Billy" Anderson—was where Francis Bushman starred in the first-ever full-length epic *Graustark* with extras including several social register types. One swell even played a chauffeur driving his own $10,000 car. Spoor couldn't have been happier about that kind of low overhead. After all, Spoor had a reputation for being tight with a dollar, even having turned away Mary Pickford in 1905 when she asked for $45 a week (yet ten years later considered himself lucky to sign Charlie Chaplin for $1,200 a week). Like everyone else, Essanay moved west, where Spoor lost $4 million in the

For an all-too-brief moment, Edgewater's Essanay Studios and other moviemakers were the center of the American cinema industry. *Photo by the author.*

Depression and the advent of "talkies." He left show biz and recouped his losses by lucky investments in Texas oil wells.

Anderson, who had been appearing in westerns since playing three different roles in the 1903 *Great Train Robbery*, eventually tried producing Broadway plays and then returned to westerns but without the "Broncho Billy" moniker he had been forced to stop using to avoid violating copyright laws.

Both men eventually received honorary Academy Awards for their "contributions to the development of motion pictures as entertainment." Anderson died in 1971 at ninety and was honored with a commemorative U.S. stamp in 1998. Spoor got his honorary Oscar in 1948 and died six years later. His accomplishments reportedly included making the first newsreel (of President William McKinley's inauguration in 1897). He was later "credited" with turning out the first fake combat coverage when he reproduced the Spanish-American War Battle of Santiago using tin soldiers, cigar smoke and neighborhood residents to help re-create Colonel Teddy Roosevelt's charge up San Juan Hill in a nearby park.

But While the Studios Are Long Gone, Filmmakers Have Stayed Busy Here

The Green Mill, for example, has been the backdrop for numerous films, including the 1991 Kathleen Turner classic *V.I. Warshawsky*, as well as *Next of Kin*, starring Patrick Swayze as a Chicago cop. Back in 1981, director and former Chicagoan Michael Mann used the then-down-at-the-heels bar for several scenes, including a spectacular bombing that all but erased a mockup covering the club's real front door and picture window. Unfortunately, the trademark "Green Mill Lounge" sign wasn't so lucky, according to Arnie Bernstein in his book *Hollywood on Lake Michigan*. The obliterated sign was quickly replaced with the exact replica you see today.

The Mill was also home for lighter fare, including *Kissing a Fool* (1998) and *Prelude to a Kiss* (1992). The club has even played an all-black bar—three times. In *Folks* (1992), Tom Selleck goes looking for his missing father, Don Ameche, and again in *A Family Thing* four years later, the club was used for a scene where Robert Duvall, a southern white who learns his mother was black, goes to hang out at the club, explaining to the regulars that he's one of them. Again in 1997, the Green Mill was the setting for *Soul Food*, the story of a black band making its big city debut.

Medium Cool, a look at the Democratic National Convention through the eyes of a TV news cameraman and an Uptown Appalachian family, even gave a shot at stardom to thirteen-year-old Harold Blankenship, who was discovered by director Haskell Wexler living with his hardscrabble family in an apartment on North Racine near Wilson Avenue.

Blankenship told *Chicago Sun-Times* reporter Charles Thegze that he almost ran away from the opportunity. "I was walking down Clifton when I came to the store to get some pop. I saw this guy [director Harold Wexler] standing by a station wagon giving out potato chips. He asked me what house my mother lived in but I took off and hid in the back yard because I thought he was a detective trying to get me. But he was making a movie and asked me if I wanted to be in it. And I said 'sure.'"

When told after the movie was finished that he could bring all his buddies when it opened in a local theater, Blankenship grinned. "Oh no. There's 5,000 of them. I'd need the whole theater."

But it wasn't long after the shooting finished that Harold Blankenship was back to his old life. After all, $300 a week didn't go very far when you've got a family to help support. "It's all gone," he shrugged a few weeks after the shooting ended.

While Harold Blankenship's future didn't change that much, he never forgot the experience. Or Haskell Wexler, who made him a star, if only for a moment. He ended up naming his first son after the director who gave him a glimpse at how the other half lives.

Even Uptown's cemeteries made the movies, Bernstein said, noting that Graceland, 4001 North Clark, was the scene for the fireman's funeral in *Backdraft* (1991) and another burial in *Damien: Omen II* (1978), right by the Potter and Bertha Palmer tombs. The iconic graveyard was also background for *The Naked Face* (1984), *The Negotiator* (1888) and the *Early Edition* TV series.

The cemetery just across Irving Park Road may be the only Jewish cemetery in Chicago used to stage Catholic graveside rites in *Running Scared* (1986). According to Bernstein, faux snow was used to cover the Hebrew inscriptions and six-pointed Stars of David carved into many of the markers.

Rosehill, 5800 North Ravenswood, was where they shot the final scenes of *Next of Kin* and some far livelier shots in *U.S. Marshals* (1998).

"CHINATOWN NORTH" OR "LITTLE SAIGON"? ARGYLE FORGING NEW IDENTITY AS "ASIAN VILLAGE"

Judge Sam Amirante stopped several feet away from Charlie Soo's flower-draped coffin and did a profound bow in a traditional Chinese gesture of respect during the "Mayor of Argyle Street's" April 2001 funeral service at Rosehill Cemetery.

"He brought Southeast Asia to the North Side of Chicago," Amirante said of the tireless civic booster who, along with restaurateur Jimmy Wong, is credited with starting the Argyle Street renaissance back in the 1970s. But most important, he did it with gentleness as well as conviction, Amirante said.

Born in Hawaii to Chinese immigrant parents, Charlie Soo came to Chicago to attend Roosevelt University and then started an import/export business. Illinois governor Otto Kerner named him to a trade mission and packed him off to Europe to promote Illinois businesses and products—and make useful future contacts like State Senator Cecil Partee, who was able to help Soo (and Argyle Street) big time after moving on to head the Chicago Department of Human Services.

Of course, not everyone appreciated Charlie Soo's aggressive promotional approach, as former 48th Ward alderman Marion Volini told the *Chicago Reader*'s Ben Joravasky: "Charlie was a hard worker, but there were people here before him. There were a lot of people who thought Charlie tried to take too much credit, that he was an outsider from Chinatown who just burst on the scene."

He also got into a donnybrook with Mayor Harold Washington's administration when his fledgling Asian American Small Business Association didn't get some funds he was promised. Soo sued, and the city withheld further money. Soo started spending money out of his own pocket to keep his programs going.

Friends say he never did get all those promised city funds, but in the end, he did get respect. "It's human kindness the world needs today. Sometimes the good are self-righteous, but the kind are always welcome everywhere," Amirante said of Soo.

Alderman Joseph Moore (49th) said Soo sacrificed his own prosperity to found and lead the Asian American Small Business Association and revitalize the once-seedy Argyle Street strip with attractions like an annual Taste of Argyle street fair and getting the Chicago Transit Authority (CTA) to invest $250,000 on a new Chinese-themed el stop all done up in jade

An elevated station with a distinctly Oriental touch greets visitors to Chicago's "new Chinatown." Or is it "Little Saigon"? Either way, "Asia on Argyle" has become a destination for a growing number of tourists and locals alike. *Photo by the author.*

green and red—Chinese good fortune colors—with the fare collection booth downstairs looking more like a miniature teahouse.

He got money from Mayor Jane Byrne to fix the decaying sidewalks and then hit up her successor, Harold Washington, for still more funds to repair the store and restaurant façades.

The "Mayor of Argyle Street" even helped get a "Chinatown North" restaurant, Sun Wah, into the Taste of Chicago, serving duck alongside Arnie Morton's Steakhouse and Eli's cheesecake.

While Charlie Soo was doing all that and more, restaurateur Jimmy Wong had been buying up properties on Argyle since the 1970s, when the small Chinese community around Clark and Van Buren led by the Hip Sing Tong was being razed to make way for a new federal detention center. Since they couldn't move back to the main Chinatown at Cermak and Wentworth because the Hip Sings had signed a contract with the On Leong Tong never to return to the old neighborhood at the end of a long tong war in the 1930s,

Wong and other community leaders looked northward. And Argyle Street wasn't much to look at back then.

In the 1880s, James Campbell, an alderman and land investor, centered his Argyle Park suburb around the new Chicago, Milwaukee & St. Paul Railway. The station was eventually linked to the Chicago elevated train network, a popular destination for limited-income people who couldn't afford to live in Edgewater.

During the post–World War II years, the street started going sleazy. Where many saw blight, Wong saw opportunity. By the late 1960s, the Hip Sing Association—like most of the old tongs—had evolved into a business and benevolent organization. Wong and his associates owned 60 percent of the properties along Argyle.

Things abruptly changed in the 1980s, when an apparently well-organized gang of thugs crashed a Chinese New Year's party, taking jewelry, wallets and watches, and then—as if to show them who's boss—forced the men to drop their pants. Shortly afterward, Jimmy Wong broke both hips in an accident and sold his Chicago properties to "pursue other opportunities" on the West Coast. Rumor has it that the Gray Ghost Shadows, a crime syndicate from the Chinese mainland, may have been involved. But the police were reportedly never able to prove anything. None of the victims at the party saw, heard or remembered much.

"The Chinese tend to keep things among themselves," Sergeant Patrick Ward, a Chicago Police Department neighborhood relations officer, said at the time, adding that what goes on in Chinatown stays in Chinatown. "And there just aren't that many Chinese Americans on this job," Ward noted.

By the early 2000s, both Charlie Soo and Jimmy Wong were dead, and Argyle's Asian commercial community faced an unforeseen identity crisis after hundreds of refugees flooded the neighborhood at the end of the Vietnam War. Was the one-time honky-tonk heaven now to become Chinatown North or Saigon West? While diversity is one of the area's strengths, it's also a challenge. Chinese and Vietnamese businesses still tend to stick to themselves, Sun Wah Restaurant manager Kelly Chang told *Chicago Tribune* reporter Naomi Nix. "We're cliquish that way. It's harder to get someone to cover all those different ethnicities under one umbrella."

While there were still some empty storefronts along Argyle in 2013, and a gunman shot one man and injured another a block from Argyle Street a year earlier, things have changed a lot for the better in recent years, business owners say. More and more tourists are coming, especially Vietnamese from as far away as Indiana, Ohio and Wisconsin, as well as the Chicago area,

Jerrod Kogan told Nix. "Where else are you going to get half a duck for $7.75?" asked Kogan, who regularly visits Argyle Street to buy ingredients like Thai basil, fried noodles and fresh fish at the ethnic groceries.

Alderman Harry Osterman has even opened a satellite ward service office on Argyle to provide programs, hold neighborhood meetings and in general reach out to local residents and merchants.

But despite all the progress, Janet Attarian, a project director at the city Department of Transportation, told Nix the Argyle business strip still needs to be "knitted together." That may prove even more challenging than ever as the street's very success attracts more new and different newcomers. "What about the Cambodians? What about the Laotians?" Chinese restaurant owner Paul Tsang asked Nix.

Others warn that if a neighborhood becomes too popular, "yuppification" could easily displace the same immigrants who built the neighborhood in the first place. "The critical question is not whether [an area] is successful or not, but who is it successful for," Euan Hague, chairman of DePaul University's geography department, told the *Tribune*.

TWENTY YEARS AFTER SAIGON'S FALL, VIET VETS WERE REMINDED TO STAND TALL AND HOLD THEIR HEADS HIGH

There were solemn rites and some tears, but no apologies, in May 1995 as American and Vietnamese veterans recalled the twentieth anniversary of the fall of Saigon, ending more than a dozen years of U.S. involvement in Southeast Asia.

"The cause was right. The mission was right," Congressman Michael Flanagan (R-5th) told more than one thousand people who marched through "Little Saigon" to the Vietnam War Museum on the 900 block of West Carmen Avenue.

"Many people both in and out of government are making a career out of apologizing for the Vietnam War," said Flanagan, himself a former army artillery captain who served in the Gulf War. But there's nothing to apologize for, he said.

"You did your part. It was the government that let you down," Flanagan told the graying ex-GIs, many of them in combat fatigues bedecked with medals and service ribbons.

But despite the way it was mishandled, the war did achieve a victory of sorts, he said. "The goal of halting the spread of Communism was ultimately realized with the razing of the Berlin War and the collapse of the Soviet Union," he said.

Former marine James Balcer, who went on to become Chicago's veterans affairs director and later 12th Ward alderman, blamed the press and the politicians for the war's outcome. "They [the North Vietnamese and their Viet Cong allies] got their butts kicked in every major battle of that war," said Balcer, noting there were far fewer Communist enclaves around the world by 1995 than there were when Communist forces stormed into Saigon.

But it's not yet time to get too comfortable, warned one-time South Vietnamese fighter pilot Kiet Vo, president of the Vietnamese Veterans Association of Illinois. "The world will never be completely safe as long as Communism exists anywhere. But it's only a matter of time before the last Communist holdouts are ousted."

A light drizzle was replaced by bright skies just ten minutes before thirty marching units stepped off at Broadway and Thorndale, concluding two days of ceremonies honoring those who served in what was then America's longest war. "We put in a requisition for good weather in triplicate and we got sun," beamed Joe Hertl, founder of the Vietnam War Museum, who had been working on plans for this observance since the previous fall.

Like other speakers, Hertl had little patience with latter-day self-recrimination by people like Robert McNamara, President Lyndon Johnson's defense secretary who had just written a book portraying Vietnam as an "unwinnable war" despite his own assurances to Americans that he saw "light at the end of the tunnel."

Hertl, who became a city building inspector after the war and was in Vietnam during the 1968 Tet Offensive, expressed hope that future U.S. leaders will have a clearer idea of what they want to accomplish the next time they send troops to fight overseas. He also hoped that politicians would leave the tactics and strategy to the professionals and make sure they at least have enough public support to last for the long haul.

After all, Hertl said, April 30, 1975, didn't just happen in a single day.

NIKE MISSILES MADE GOOD NEIGHBORS ON LAKEFRONT DURING COLD WAR, BUT WERE THEY ALREADY OBSOLETE?

With apologies to the late Johnny Cash, Montrose Harbor was once part of Chicago's own "Ring of Fire" during the Cold War. From 1955 to 1965, both the Belmont and Montrose Harbor lakefronts were largely underground Nike-Ajax antiaircraft missile bases.

"Chicago is loaded for bear—even the Russian bear if the Reds should ever dare to send their bombers to attack the city," trumpeted an editorial in the *Chicago American*. "They [the Nikes] are inescapable by any air maneuver now known to aviation. They make nice neighbors."

The dart-like missiles were often in plain sight but could be retracted into underground bunkers and moved into firing position as needed.

Contrary to urban myth, however, the Nikes—with their twenty-five-mile range—couldn't be aimed at Moscow, Leningrad or even Havana but were designed only to shoot down approaching enemy bombers. So when neighborhood leaders began complaining about the use of public parkland for missile sites, the Nikes were already obsolete. While most of the sites were out in the boonies, the ones around Montrose Harbor were only a short distance from lakefront high-rises.

Ironically, the Montrose missile base probably got more attention *after* it was deactivated, when a handful of Indians demonstrated solidarity with their Lakota Sioux brethren during the 1971 standoff with federal agents at the Wounded Knee, South Dakota reservation. Inside the abandoned base, Indian spokesman Mike Chosa vowed to stand up to the dozens of police waiting only a few hundred yards away. "My heart leaps like an eagle," Chosa told a reporter as he watched the "bluecoats" moving into position, preparing to put down what looked like Chicago's first Indian "uprising" in more than 150 years. "Any day is a good day to die," said Chosa, who had obviously seen the movie *Little Big Man* making the rounds of local theaters that summer.

But by early July, after a siege lasting several weeks, police and park workers rounded up some fifty Indians during a predawn raid censured that very evening by the Lake View Citizens Council (LVCC). Ned Ganz, chairman of the LVCC's Nike Site Committee, said the forcible eviction solved none of the issues that led the Indians to take over the missile site in the first place.

Deputy Chief of Patrol Robert Lynsky later said police never intended to move the Indians out but only to protect work crews being brought in to tear down the seven-foot-high chain-link fence surrounding the army installation. The plan changed, Lynsky said, when the Indians resisted with clubs, bricks, bottles and even firebombs, one of which destroyed a $10,000 boat moored in the harbor.

Mystery-Ridden Rainbo Gardens Kept Reinventing Itself for Nearly a Century

The now long-gone Rainbo Skating Rink, 4812 North Clark, may well be a top contender for the North Side's most recycled building, with its own dark secrets, such as how an assortment of still unidentified human bones and gym shoes ended up in the basement.

The grim discovery was made when the building was being demolished in 2002 to make way for a new town house/condo development on the site of the Mann's Million Dollar Rainbo Room, so named because impresario Frank Mann called it the Rainbo Room recalling his World War I service in France with the U.S. Army's 42nd Infantry, better known as the Rainbow Division. According to legend, Mann and his partners invested $1 million in the early 1920s to make the Rainbo the country's biggest nightclub. The Rainbo Room had table seating for 2,000 patrons, dance floor spaces for 1,500 and a revolving stage for nonstop entertainment.

Actor Larry Fine was working here in 1934 when he was invited to join the Three Stooges. Until 1927, WMAQ radio shared the same frequency with station WGJ owned by both the Rainbo and Calumet Baking Powder, which broadcast live music from the Rainbo Room as a promotional tool. That same year, at the height—or depths—of Prohibition, the Rainbo Room was converted into a casino and sports venue and renamed the Rainbo Fronton.

Seven years later, during the Chicago Century of Progress World's Fair, the Rainbo got a French theme, and on June 22, 1934, bank robber John Dillinger celebrated his last birthday exactly a month before he was shot leaving the Biograph Theater on Lincoln Avenue. In 1939, the Rainbo became Mike Todd's Theater Café, a popular dance theater where choreographer Tommy Sutton worked with Nat King Cole, Cab Calloway and Duke Ellington.

Sixteen years later, the Rainbo hosted the first women's tag-team wrestling matches. Three years later, the Mike Todd Theater Café was converted into an ice rink used for practice by the Chicago Blackhawks (including when they won the 1961 Stanley Cup). The Rainbo was also used for training

Olympic figure skaters, had a professional-level bowling alley and became home to the first Kinetic Playground music hall.

From the 1960s until it was razed for the Rainbo Village housing development, one of the city's best-known playgrounds for grown-ups evolved into a popular late-night roller rink. One can only wonder what the Rainbo's next reincarnation might have been.

History Sometimes Seemed Better Second Time Around

Over the years, history has had a habit of literally repeating itself in Uptown and Edgewater. It was, as they say, "déjà vu all over again" for local resident Walter Kallas and the hundreds of other D-Day vets who packed the bleachers at Montrose Beach in early June 1994 for a reenactment of the Normandy Invasion.

Half a century earlier, Kallas, who went on to become proprietor of Wally's Grocery, 3609 West Montrose, was a staff sergeant with the Ninety-second Chemical Mortar Battalion. The Bronze Star recipient not only survived the Longest Day but also went through four other major battles, including the Bulge.

He counted himself especially lucky to have been around for D-Day Plus 50. Not long after Normandy, the army offered him a choice between a promotion to second lieutenant or a thirty-day leave. He took the furlough, and when he returned, he found 75 percent of his unit had been wiped out.

Chicago's World War II Commemorative Committee, the U.S. Navy and the Historical Reenactment Society had worked for most of 1993 to make the largest D-Day reenactment this side of France as realistic as possible. Accompanied by reporters dressed as World War II combat correspondents, some four hundred reenactors in authentic World War II battle gear stormed ashore from five assault craft as fifteen vintage aircraft, including B-25 bombers, softened up one hundred or so "Germans" holding the beachhead.

Before it was over, the reenactment at times turned out to be far more realistic than even the organizers had planned. Like when one of the navy landing craft had to unload its troops in nearly five feet of surf that proved so rough one man lost his rifle. Or when a smaller boat ferrying the "British" and "Canadian" contingents started taking on water.

Warren Berry, a Chicago policeman when he wasn't a chief warrant officer in the U.S. Navy Reserve, had professional reasons for wanting to go along for a ride on one of the landing craft. An amphibious assault specialist assigned to a unit at Great Lakes Naval Training Center, Berry wanted to see what his job would have been like half a century earlier. If the Normandy Invasion had taken place in 1994, he said, casualties would have been a lot lighter because the landings would have been done much differently, with equipment like helicopters and hovercraft that wasn't even dreamed of in 1944.

Others on the boats, like Sam Henner of Richfield, Ohio, another veteran, said World War II may someday be as popular with reenactors as the Civil War. "But not now. Not enough time has passed yet," Henner said. "The memory is still too fresh in too many people's minds."

In fact, the 1994 redux wouldn't have come about if 46th Ward alderman Helen Shiller had her way. "Not on My Beach" screamed a headline paraphrasing the often-controversial city council member's concerns that the event would be a traffic, parking and crowd control nightmare. Shiller was overruled, and D-Day II went off without any serious snags.

Another historic reenactment came two years later at Rosehill Cemetery for those who missed Abraham Lincoln's funeral the first time.

On April 14, 1995, the 130th anniversary of the Great Emancipator's assassination, period dirges played by regimental bands of Civil War reenactors and a uniformed honor guard escorted an exact replica of Lincoln's coffin (with a Lincoln impersonator inside) from the front gate to the cemetery chapel—just the way it would have happened if it were not for a last-minute change in plans, according to then Rosehill historian David Wendell.

According to Wendell at least, the Lincoln family originally planned to have the burial at Rosehill because of Lincoln's often-expressed wish to retire in Chicago after leaving the White House. In the days after the assassination, Chicago and Springfield fought for the honor of being Lincoln's final resting place, with Springfield winning only after Springfield's movers and shakers hastily raised $100,000 for a temporary tomb.

The funeral reenactment, which was to be filmed for a *Civil War Journal* episode on cable TV's Arts and Entertainment channel, drew more than one thousand participants in period costumes and several thousand spectators. Pallbearers wearing the same type of light blue uniforms worn by the Veterans Reserve Corps that escorted the funeral train from Washington to Springfield were selected by Wendell from among men descended from people connected in some way with Lincoln or his assassination. One was related to Dr. Samuel Mudd, who was imprisoned for setting John Wilkes Booth's broken leg, even though he didn't know his patient had shot the president. Another was related to one of the officers in charge of the detail that cornered Booth at Garrett's Farm. Still another made the cut for being more-than-friends with a great-grandniece of Mary Todd Lincoln.

The reenactment also featured what Wendell described as the largest-ever collection of Lincoln funeral memorabilia, including part of the wreath laid on the president's chest and a swatch from Mrs. Lincoln's mourning dress. A 1⁄12-scale model of the Lincoln funeral train went on display at Rosehill after a brief ceremony attended by James Gormley and William Becker, descendants of two of the engineers who drove the train.

Wendell liked to say that during his time as the cemetery's historian, he brought more people to Rosehill than all the wars and plagues of the previous century. And he may not have been exaggerating that much. When Rosehill marked the 125th anniversary of its first burial (of a doctor named Jacob Ludlam) in 1994, Wendell arranged for a one-day visit by the Illinois Funeral Directors Association's traveling museum. The museum-on-wheels' displays included items like nineteenth-century embalming tools, mortuary cosmetics, a photo of a white horse-drawn children's hearse and a return visit by the replica of Abraham Lincoln's coffin (made by the same company that built the original for $1,500 in 1865). Also on display was a copy of President Kennedy's $12,000 mahogany casket, which Wendell said was encased in a metal vault. The cast-iron Fisk Caskets, which made their debut in the 1850s, were "probably the closest thing to immortality," Wendell said. So were the ice coffins used to help the departed travel better. For truly stylish departures, Wendell pointed out a sporty little dark wood model that went for only $50 when it was made back in 1880.

Also featured were nineteenth-century curios like the metal coverings used to keep the deceased's eyes closed, a special plate nailed on the coffin of women who died of breast cancer, "mourning spoons" that were chewed on by the grief-stricken and jewelry made of the loved one's hair. Long before photography was commonplace, Wendell said, some mourners wove strands of the deceased's hair with that of other dead relatives in a kind of family album. There was also a mourning band intended to be torn up by Orthodox Jews who didn't want to have to rend their clothing, as prescribed by religious law. Wendell ended Rosehill's 125th anniversary observance with a Victorian picnic complete with bands, carriage rides and an "appearance" by President and Mrs. Lincoln.

That year, Wendell also held a June 14 ceremony marking the centennial of Flag Day with a brief ceremony at the grave of Edward Bigelow, the North Sider credited with starting the holiday by bringing four thousand children to a rally in Lincoln Park.

The previous year, Wendell organized the dedication of new gravestones for the more than one hundred Civil War dead buried near Rosehill's fortress-like front gate.

He held events honoring the only Chicagoan killed on the Hindenburg and a Fourth of July celebration complete with the "1812 Overture" and personally gave a stirring oration lauding Alexander I for standing up to Napoleon. It was probably one of the few times a speaker at a July 4 ceremony stopped just short of calling a Russian czar a freedom fighter!

So why did Wendell keep trying to lure people into a graveyard before their time? Partly because, until recently, cemeteries were as much for the living as the dead, said the self-taught historian who conducted tours of the cemetery, which he called "the last stop for all of us."

Rosehill's management apparently had no problem until Wendell announced plans to hold a "hot dog day" at the grave of Oscar Meyer, with a procession led by the Weinermobile and groups of kids singing "I Wish I Were an Oscar Meyer Weiner." That was too much even for Rosehill.

Wendell's job was soon eliminated, and the mini–Civil War museum he set up in the cemetery office became history.

The Day the Irish Fight for Freedom Found Its Way to an Uptown Sewer

Chicago got a taste of the Irish "Troubles" up close and personal in May 1889 with the still-unsolved murder of Dr. Patrick Cronin. The naked body of the respected physician and Irish independence activist was found stuffed in a sewer near what is now Broadway and Foster. All he was wearing was the religious medal he always wore around his neck.

Cronin was last seen grabbing his medical bag and leaving with a stranger in a carriage the evening of May 4. That visitor was overheard telling the doctor a workman had been run over by a wagon and needed immediate help.

Two days later, Lake View police found a bloodstained traveling trunk containing hairs believed to be Cronin's in a wooded area not far from what is now the Broadway and Montrose intersection.

On May 23, after newspapers as far away as New York City began running stories about Cronin's disappearance or possible flight to Canada, Cronin's corpse was found by city sewer workers checking out complaints about a clogged catch basin not far from the Argyle Park railroad station. Hundreds of Irish nationalists filed through the morgue that evening paying their respects.

After a hero's funeral at Holy Name Cathedral, Cronin was buried with full honors at Calvary Cemetery. Nearly eight thousand men representing a variety of organizations—including the Ancient Order of Hibernians and the Catholic Foresters—along with several militia units including the Sheridan Guards, four drum corps and a full marching band provided the escort.

But nobody ever found out who killed Cronin—and why.

One theory was that Cronin was about to blow the whistle on an embezzlement scheme involving some top leaders of *Clan na Gael*, a secret Irish revolutionary group Cronin may have had ties to at one point. Another is that the people Cronin was about to name retaliated by accusing Cronin of being a paid spy working for Thomas Beach (alias Henri LeCaron), one of four British agents trying to infiltrate Feinian groups in Chicago and other major U.S. and Canadian cities. That, of course, set Cronin up for retaliation by *Clan na Gael* and other groups that had been collecting money, weapons and volunteers to take the uprising to England itself.

The police investigation led by Inspector Michael Schaak of the East Chicago Avenue police district—who had no love for the Irish—arrested and questioned some three hundred suspects, even including some prominent business and society leaders known to be sympathetic to the Irish cause.

A grand jury quickly indicted the inner circle of *Clan na Gael*. The first Cronin murder trial—rampant with charges of jury tampering and bias against the Irish in general—ended with guilty verdicts against four defendants: John Kunze, Martin Burke, Patrick O'Sullivan and Dan Coughlan, the East Chicago Avenue District cop who allegedly drew the lot to carry out Cronin's "execution." Coughlin appealed his conviction and was acquitted in 1894. A throng of waiting supporters cheered him as he left the criminal court/county jail complex (now a luxury condo building).

Later that day, wreaths were placed on the graves of Burke and O'Sullivan, both of whom had died in Joliet Prison. Another defendant, Patrick "the Fox" Cooney, fled before he could be brought to trial and was never seen again.

Detective Coughlin began a new career as a Chicago saloonkeeper.

Still never explained after all these years was why Cronin's killers left that holy medal on his neck after stripping him of everything else. Lake View mayor Billy Boldenweck, however, surmised the killers were obviously "too religious" to go that far.

"Lincoln Park Pirates" Now Heave To on Clark Street

Although nobody is exactly bragging about it, Edgewater is also the home of the notorious Lincoln Towing Service, immortalized in Steve Goodman's 1972 hit song "Lincoln Park Pirates" about ex-con Ross Cascio's buccaneer-like business practices. The controversial company at 4882 North Clark (with a satellite location at 4601 West Armitage), whose official name is the Protective Parking Corporation, has described itself as an auto "relocater" that protects property owners from illegal parkers on sites with Lincoln Towing contracts. Folk singer Goodman got no radio play because stations were afraid of lawsuits because the "Pirates" song mentioned Cascio by name. That changed when Cascio let it be known he was proud of the song, that it was virtually an unpaid commercial for Lincoln Towing.

While there have been numerous towing services in Chicago, this one became especially infamous in the 1960s and '70s when the late columnist Mike Royko began taking Cascio to task for his alleged "strong-arm" service style. Alderman Dick Simpson (44th) and James Kargman, one of Simpson's opponents in the 1971 race, both made the company a campaign issue. Kargman promised to "hit Cascio in the wallet, where it hurts," calling on businesses to cancel their contracts with Lincoln Towing. Cascio told one reporter that most of the businesses that dropped Lincoln Towing promised Cascio they'd re-up after the election, when the political heat was off.

But the heat didn't get turned off. After the election, an estimated three hundred people mobbed a Lincoln Towing employee who was trying to impound an illegally parked car. At one point, the city council considered cracking down on Lincoln Towing. But that was easier said than done.

Cascio and his successors have insisted all the while that they're a legitimate business, operating well within the laws. Asked about his penchant for hiring ex-offenders, Cascio told a North Side neighborhood newspaper reporter in the mid-1970s that even guys who have done time deserve a second chance.

In 1992, Lincoln Towing, then being run by Steve Mash, was charged with possession of stolen cars after police saw Mash's employees tow a car that was later seen being stripped for parts that were sold for scrap. Lincoln Towing and Mash were eventually acquitted.

Illinois Commerce Commission officials told the *Chicago Tribune* that while Lincoln Towing had 2,078 complaints between 2000 and 2005, that wasn't much different from similar businesses operating in Illinois. During that same time, Lincoln Towing gave 139 full refunds, which the ICC said compared with other companies.

Was Prepaid Healthcare Born at Sailors' Hospital?

Long before anyone ever heard of HMOs or national health insurance, sailors were paying forty cents a month in premiums to qualify for treatment at the old Merchant Marine Hospital at 4141 North Clarendon. From 1873 until the early 1970s, when the ten-acre site was leased to Walt Disney Magnet School, the old U.S. Public Health Service center served as a "refuge for those following the seafaring life" and was eventually treating a dozen other categories of patients, including federal employees injured on duty and World War I veterans.

The $450,000 facility was Chicago's third sailors' hospital since 1852, when then-congressman "Long John" Wentworth led a campaign to convert the old Fort Dearborn site—now the 300 block of North Michigan Avenue—into a hospital for Great Lakes sailors run by Dr. Ralph Isham.

As many as one thousand Civil War casualties a year passed through the cramped thirty-six-room clinic, which was later sold to the Michigan Central Railroad and replaced with a new center at Rush Street and the river. During the Chicago fire, Dr. Niles Quales, deserted by his entire staff except for two nurses, managed to save all sixty-seven patients in that hospital, including two with broken legs.

But by then, work had already started on the 350-bed "suburban" Lake View hospital, despite objections from staffers who didn't relish daily six-

Ravenswood and Bryn Mawr, 1920s.

mile carriage commutes over bumpy, almost nonexistent roads. By July 1885, however, Dr. John Benson was treating 300 people in the new dispensary and another 150 in the hospital itself for ailments including smallpox and contagious fevers. That month, 70 were discharged as cured and 3 died—an incredibly low mortality rate in an era when inpatients were more likely to die of infections than from the injuries or illnesses that brought them to the hospital in the first place.

Of course, the sailors themselves must have been an exceptionally healthy breed, if the early records are to be believed. The same year, for example, hospital surgeons examined 192 would-be Great Lakes pilots for colorblindness, and only 2 flunked the test. They also gave the required annual physicals to Chicago-based members of the Life Saving Service (a forerunner of today's U.S. Coast Guard). Everybody passed!

"Children's Poet" Eugene Field Proudly Claimed by Uptown as Well as Lake View

If Edgewater had its modern Michelangelo, whom we shall meet later, Uptown had its own poet laureate, especially for children: Eugene Field, who, unlike most bards, was neither poor nor unknown even while he was alive. He apparently also had what the Irish call "second sight."

Clark Street north of Foster Avenue, 1920s.

The Clark/Ridge Tavern, early 1900s.

In early November 1895, as he was packing for a lecture trip in Kansas City, the already world-renowned literary light mused to nobody in particular that "this is the dying time of the year." The next morning, the forty-five-year-old author of "Wynken, Blynken and Nod," considered by some critics to be the best children's poem ever written in the English language, was found dead of an apparent heart attack by his thirteen-year-old son, Fred "Daisy" at what is now 4240 North Clarendon Avenue.

Word of his death spread almost instantly. Crowds flocked to the "Sabine Farm," which is what Field called his rambling white mansion in then-suburban Buena Park bounded by Montrose, Graceland Cemetery, Irving Park and Lake Shore Drive right on the border between Lake View and Uptown.

His passing brought tributes from admirers across the globe, ranging from fellow bard Joel Chandler Harris to a crippled boy who showed up at Field's home asking for a farewell look at the "Children's Poet" whose "Sharps and Flats" in the *Chicago Record* had also helped establish the personal opinion column as a mainstay of modern newspapers.

He'd served his apprenticeship as a reporter and editor in St. Louis, Kansas City and Denver after bumming around in Europe squandering an inheritance mostly on curios, including a robe he bought from a Japanese Shinto priest just so he'd be the only one in America to have one. But he had an uncanny way of replenishing his cash reserves. He even turned a profit on one of his hobbies with "Affairs of a Bibliomaniac," a humorous dissertation on his adventures in book collecting. He collected his front-porch thoughts in his 1892 *Echoes of Sabine Farm* when he wasn't collaborating with his brother, Roswell, on a rhymed translation of the works of the Roman poet Horace.

While few topics were off limits to gadfly Field, his favorites seem to have been the cultural pretensions of Chicago's meat barons (he later put those columns in a book, *Culture's Garland*) and unreliable public transportation ("The oldest horse in Chicago works for the Lake View Street Car Co. and was present at the Battle of Marathon in 490 B.C.").

Despite a rewarding career poking fun at pomp and privilege, even the Union League Club sent a wreath to his standing room–only funeral at Fourth Presbyterian Church, where the hymns included "Singing in God's Acre," written by Field himself. Old friend Frank Gunaslus delivered the eulogy entirely in verse.

Mourners ranged from *Chicago Daily News* publisher Victor Lawson to classmates of Field's two sons at Alcott School, 2625 North Orchard Street. Floral pieces included a broken pen, drum and trumpet commemorating

Field's second-best-known poem, "Little Boy Blue," and a single flower that was all one little factory urchin could afford.

Not surprisingly, Field was soon honored with both a school (at 7019 North Ashland Avenue) and a monument built in 1922 just east of Lincoln Park Zoo's Small Animal House. Years later, city architect Ira Bach called that monument unique in that "it doesn't scare children like some statues do." Eugene Field would have been pleased.

Sage of Castlewood Terrace Had "Life Well Lived"

For at least twenty years, author, activist and radio personality Studs Terkel held quiet court in spacious surroundings on the 900 block of West Castlewood Terrace. Some would say this was an unlikely place for a proletarian writer, radio host and sometime activist to spend his sunset years. Not that there was anything bucolic about Terkel's so-called sunset years. Lying next to his deathbed was his latest book, *P.S. or Thoughts from a Lifetime of Listening*, scheduled for release that month. He was ninety-six.

His was "a long, satisfying and fulfilling but tempestuous life," his son Dan told reporters after his funeral. "It was a life well lived."

In fact, it was hard to imagine a fuller life, said Rick Kogan in Louis "Studs" Terkel's *Chicago Tribune* obituary. "Television institution for years, radio staple for decades, and a literary lion since 1967 when he wrote his first best-selling book at age 55." His life was full of stories. Like the time he refused to cross an informational picket line to go into the "Purple Hotel" in Lincolnwood to receive the Lerner Newspapers' "Citizen of the Year" award after learning of a dispute between the paper's management and the Chicago Newspaper Guild. Or the time he went over to the Sulzer Regional Library to lend moral support to staff trying to save hundreds of books ordered ditched because the then–library commissioner had labeled them "obsolete." Among them were the Koran and some of the works of Mark Twain.

Born in New York City in 1912, he would often say, "I came up when the *Titanic* went down." He came to Chicago when his parents bought the Wells-Grand Hotel, a virtual flophouse that Terkel recalls housed a colorful variety of people who enriched his understanding of the real world.

Marchers in one of Andersonville's many parades.

He supplemented his life experience with visits to Bughouse Square just across the street from the Newberry Library at Clark and Walton, then home to all manner of soapbox orators ranging from Carl Sandburg and Clarence Darrow to "One Arm Charlie" Wendorf and Eddie Lamaka, whose only cause was Kenya's independence from Britain. "I doubt whether I learned very much at the park. I know I delighted in it. Perhaps none of it made any sense save one thing—a sense of life," he recalled. Years later, Terkel himself emceed the annual Bughouse Square Debates until a variety of ailments, including being virtually deaf, forced him to relinquish the honor that eventually went to Rick Kogan.

Although he graduated from the prestigious University of Chicago Law School, Terkel never actually practiced law. Since it was the Depression, he got a job at a federally sponsored statistical project run by the U.S. Emergency Rehabilitation Administration, one of FDR's many New Deal agencies.

He later moved on to the WPA's Writers' Project, creating plays and radio soap operas when he wasn't honing his acting talents or doubling as a sportscaster or disc jockey. The first radio program he could call his own was *The Wax Museum*, featuring selections from whatever struck his fancy, including the first recordings of gospel singer Mahalia Jackson, who later became a friend of his.

When television appeared in American homes in the early 1950s, Terkel created and hosted *Studs' Place*, one of the major glories of the Chicago School of Television that also spawned Dave Garroway and the *Kukla, Fran & Ollie* kids' show. But it was *Studs' Place*, set in a tavern, where large numbers of fans discovered what Terkel did best: talk and listen. "Arms waving, words exploding in bursts, leaning close to his talking companions, he didn't merely conduct interviews, but engaged in conversations," said Kogan.

He was interested in what he was talking about and who he was talking with, but his TV life was short. Terkel later lamented that the medium's commercialization forced his show—and the rest of the Chicago School—off the air.

By that time, McCarthyism was becoming a potent threat to anyone even a little liberal. And Terkel was very liberal. He said, "I was blacklisted because I took certain positions on things and never retracted. I signed many petitions for unfashionable causes and I never retracted." Times got tough for a lot of like-minded people. And they got to be very tough at times for Studs Terkel.

Sidney Lewis and other friends credit his longtime wife, Ida, with being his rock. "She was on every level his most important audience."

Studs Terkel finally found his place in 1952 at WFMT, where his mix of music, especially jazz and folk songs, and conversations was a perfect fit.

Then he found another career in the mid-1960s when a British actress liked his interview style and asked book publisher Andre Schffren to talk to Terkel about publishing some of his interviews. After much coaxing, Terkel wrote *Division Street America* to rave reviews in 1967. It told the stories of ordinary working people as well as businessmen, prostitutes, security guards, Hispanics and blacks who formed the divisions of society, using Chicago's Division Street as a prototype of America itself.

Terkel used the same format in *Hard Times*, about Depression-era America (1970), and *Working*, another look at ordinary people in 1974, followed by *American Dreams: Lost and Found* (1980) and *The Good War: Remembrances of World War II*, which won a 1985 Pulitzer Prize.

Most of his books were "written radio," Kogan said. "He asked the questions and they answered. He drew things out of people they didn't even know they had in them."

Asked what he'd like to do in retirement, Terkel snorted, "I think of myself as an old-time craftsman. I've been doing this five days a week for more than 30 years. When I realize the work is slipping, I'll quit. But I don't think I've reached that point yet. I still have my enthusiasms. I still love what I do."

After his wife's death, he wrote *Will the Circle Be Unbroken: Reflections on Death, Rebirth and Hunger for Faith* (2001) and *Hope Dies Last: Keeping the Faith in Difficult Times* (2003).

In the end, he wanted to be cremated, have his ashes mixed with his wife's (which he kept on his bedroom dresser) and have their cremains scattered at Bughouse Square. Reminded that would be illegal, Terkel told Kogan, "So let them sue us."

Studs' Neighbors Included Auto Bumper Critters Creator John Kearney

Just on the next block from *Studs' Place* is the home of sculptor John Kearney. Even if you're not an art aficionado, chances are you've seen his often-playful sculptures made of auto bumpers in the Edgewater/Uptown area like the big cats at Goudy School, 5720 North Winthrop; the gorilla at Uptown Hull House, 4520 North Beacon; or a life-size Kodiak bear in front of an Andersonville home. In other parts of the city, places like Oz Park feature scrap-metal renderings of the Tin Man, Cowardly Lion and Dorothy and Toto; or the "Starving Bitch" and a "Tree of Life" in the Museum of Contemporary Art.

The prolific Kearney produced hundreds of sculptures now on display everywhere, including the private collections of actress Brigitte Bardot, TV host Johnny Carson, actor Kirk Douglas, author Norman Mailer (an old friend from when they both lived around Cape Cod) and Studs Terkel (his neighbor from the next block).

Kearney reportedly has had as much as twelve to fourteen tons of auto bumpers in warehouses on the East Coast and in his Chicago studio. But since it takes an estimated one thousand pounds of bumpers to make one one-hundred-pound sculpture, Kearney once estimated that stockpile wouldn't last more than five years, if that.

Born in Omaha, Nebraska, Kearney may be the only notable American artist who learned his welding skills doing underwater repair of damaged naval ships during World War II. After four years in the U.S. Navy, he did more conventional art studies at the Cranbrook Academy in Bloomfield Hills, Michigan, and at the Universita per Stranieri in Perugia, Italy.

In 1949, after returning to the United States, he co-founded the Contemporary Art Workshop (CAW) in the old Cyrus McCormick mansion's carriage building on the Gold Coast. The CAW, which billed itself as the country's first artist-created gallery, closed in 2009 after a solid sixty-year run.

THE DAY AN EX-GI NAMED JOE DECIDED TO LIFT THE IRON CURTAIN HIMSELF

The Cold War took a rare breather for about twelve minutes in January 1959 when forty-one-year-old CTA bus driver Joe Polowsky talked peace and understanding with Deputy Soviet Premier Anastas Mikoyan in Polowsky's $97.50-a-month, four-room apartment at 4126 North Sheridan Road.

Polowsky, an infantryman who witnessed the Soviet/American linkup at the Elbe in the waning days of World War II, never forgot that moment and vowed to devote the rest of his life to promoting amity between the two superpowers that more than once had teetered on the brink of war.

When the number two Head Red said he wanted to meet an ordinary American working-class family during a fact-finding tour of the United States, Polowsky saw his chance. He invited Mikoyan over for a visit, and Mikoyan accepted.

As police sirens screeched outside their Uptown apartment building, Polowsky's Irish-born wife, Marie, grew uneasy. "I hope you know what you're doing," she whispered as Mikoyan, followed by Soviet ambassador Mikhali Menshikov and eight other Russians, a U.S. state department security detail, Chicago police and a gaggle of reporters, made his way to the family's twelve- by fourteen-foot living room.

"With a warm heart, I greet you sir. Here is Ben," Polowsky said, holding his two-year-old son. "His grandparents were born in Russia."

Behind him, holding their other child, one-year-old Irene, Mrs. Polowsky whispered, "Don't talk too much, Joe."

Mikoyan sat on a couch holding Ben, who grabbed at a TV microphone as a British-accented Russian interpreter began translating his boss's comments.

"Mr. Mikoyan feels it is his duty to meet a responsible warrior of the American people," interpreter O.A. Troyanovsky said.

"One should not forget the cooperation that existed in the war," Troyanovsky continued.

Polowsky said he was "sure it will be remembered by our grandchildren.

"May his [Mikoyan's] grandchildren and my grandchildren meet together sometime in peace and understanding," said Polowsky, adding that "both countries suffered so much in World War II. Can all this be in vain?"

He then outlined plans for an annual series of "Elbe Awards" for young people in Russia and the United States whose fathers died in the war, for disabled veterans and a student essay contest and requested Mikoyan to ask that Khrushchev serve as the program's co-chairman.

"I will ask President Eisenhower if you'll ask Mr. Khrushchev," Polowsky promised.

"You have a very interesting idea. It should be discussed," Mikoyan said just before Polowsky took Mikoyan on a tour of what he described as a "typical American worker's apartment," showing off his electric refrigerator and the two bedrooms, one of which used to be the dining room.

Outside on Sheridan Road where police had halted traffic and sealed off the block, hundreds waited nearby to see Mikoyan and his party head off for their next engagement, unaware of the earlier scuffle between police and press when Detective Chief Patrick Deeley tried to limit the number of reporters going into Polowsky's apartment.

Before his Chicago visit was over, Mikoyan would see his share of scuffles at several places where he was to speak. But the smooth-talking Mikoyan wasn't fazed by any of it. "I attach no importance to them," Mikoyan told reporters through his interpreter at the Conrad Hilton Hotel. "These handfuls do not represent the American people." The sometimes jeering, egg-throwing protests, he added, "were more like comedies than demonstrations."

Early "Megachurch" Was Once Country's Largest

Another Uptown landmark, People's Church, 941 West Lawrence, is the brainchild of one-time fundamentalist Dr. Preston Bradley, who had to start his own church in 1912 to avoid feeling like an outcast. Questioning the then–widely accepted belief that infants who died before baptism couldn't get into heaven, Bradley took eighty-six of his parishioners with him as he broke with the Presbyterian Church he'd joined after being kicked out

A classroom at St. Ita's School back in the 1910s.

of Moody Bible Institute for smoking and being seen at a movie theater. Bradley never looked back.

If the seminary teachers considered smoking shocking, we can only imagine how much their blood pressure went up when they heard his thoughts on sexual morality. "I am old fashioned enough to believe in virginity and chastity before marriage, but I do not consider variations of that code to be sinful in the sense that God will inflict everlasting punishment…Sexual force and sexual desire are natural things," he said, by then apparently blissfully unconcerned what other religious leaders thought.

"I am thoroughly, completely, adequately, gloriously and triumphantly a heretic," he trumpeted as he announced the founding of his own denomination in 1912 and began holding services at the Viking Temple on Sheffield Avenue. His congregation outgrew the space after only a month and by 1914 was renting the Wilson Avenue Theater on Sundays and then the Pantheon cinema on Sheridan Road, at that time Chicago's largest movie house until the advent of the Uptown Theater.

Originally dubbed the Uptown Temple, the People's Church at 941 West Lawrence had—as Bradley put it—"none of the architectural trappings of bygone ecclesiastical attitudes. There is no tower, no medieval chancels and naves." In their place, Bradley opted for "an open room, airy, warm, inviting fellowship and the breezes of fresh ideas." Instead of the traditional pulpit, Bradley went with a simple lectern, flanked on one side by a bust of Abraham Lincoln and Ralph Waldo Emerson on the other.

In 1923, Bradley and his followers joined the Unitarian movement, which had few objections to one of its ministers marching with Jane Addams in a women's suffrage parade, speaking out against the Ku Klux Klan and Hitler or backing FDR's New Deal.

By the 1940s, church membership had skyrocketed to about four thousand parishioners, most of whom had joined expressly to hear Bradley. According to some estimates, People's Church was at one point the country's largest nondenominational congregation. By the time of Bradley's death in 1983, six years after he retired, Sunday attendance had dropped to fifty.

Bradley became one of the country's first radio preachers, a founder of the Izak Walton Conservation League, a member of the Chicago Public Library board and the author of nine books. "I always wanted to help people meet the problems of everyday life, help people to lead creative, positive, happy lives," he once said, conceding that impulse could have led him along any number of career paths. Although he'd started out studying law back in Flint, Michigan, Bradley later admitted he couldn't remember a time when he didn't want to be a preacher or an actor.

Or a politician, some hoped. Bradley turned down two chances to run for mayor, insisting his efforts would be better spent in the pulpit or on the library board, where he once threatened Mayor William Hale Thompson with arrest if he ever made good on his campaign promise to remove all British books from the library shelves. In a bid for the Irish and German vote, "Big Bill" (or "Kaiser Bill," as he was called during World War I) then threatened to deck England's King George V if he ever set foot in Chicago.

By the end of Bradley's sixty-five-year career, however, the one-time "rebel" minister had become one of Chicago's most highly respected clerics. At a 1972 banquet in Bradley's honor, John Cardinal Cody called him "one of Chicago's greatest," while another churchman dubbed him "the Babe Ruth of his profession." None of those present, incidentally, remembered the names of any of their colleagues who just sixty years earlier had wanted to try Bradley for heresy and run him out of town.

Along the way, Bradley had become Chicago's first preacher to deliver weekly radio sermons, which Senn High School graduate Irna Phillips said inspired her to create *The Guiding Light* radio and TV serial about the trials and triumphs of a minister who always left a light burning in his study to guide anyone seeking his help. Television historians believe that one of the characters may have had the first on-air out-of-wedlock baby birth. Phillips said the series was based on her own experience as a pregnant nineteen-year-old whose boyfriend abandoned her and whose baby ultimately miscarried.

The one-time teenage outcast eventually went on to become "Queen of the Soap Operas," churning out radio/TV serials like *Road of Life*, *Woman in White*, *Young Doctor Malone* and *As the World Turns*. Her first show, *Painted Dreams*, premiered on WGN radio in 1930 as the first daytime serial aimed especially at female audiences. In 1949, *The Guiding Light* became the first radio soap adapted for TV. Its seventy-year record run on radio and TV makes it the third-longest-running program in the history of broadcasting.

Over the years, People's Church's famously non-ideological congregation hosted some unlikely programs—even a talk in the early 1970s by former Uptown community organizer and "Chicago Seven" defendant Rennie Davis, who by then had become a spokesman for the Divine Light Mission founder Guru Maharj Ji, hailed at the time as the "Perfect Master." Nearly at the point of joyous tears, Davis explained he was "blessed out," serving Guru Maharj Ji, whom he called "the greatest event in history." "If we knew who he was, we would crawl across America on our hands and knees to rest our heads at his feet," he said. Davis, the would-be revolutionary turned apostle, eventually went into business for himself as a kind of vedic venture capitalist and high-priced lecturer on meditation and self-realization. His Foundation for a New Humanity focuses on "breakthrough technology" development and investments.

In recent years, People's Church's membership evaporated in the wake of wholesale displacement as Uptown gentrified. But instead of pulling the plug, the congregation became affiliated with the United Church of Christ without severing its ties to the Unitarian-Universalist Association. Church facilities have been leased to a variety of theater groups, including the National Pastime Theater's 2013 Naked July Festival, featuring a celebration of the nude human form in art, dance and drama—including a hands-on primer in nude figure drawing.

Chicago's Little-Known Black First Lady Spent Her Last Days in an Uptown Nursing Home

Fred Busse, Chicago's first German American mayor, may have set more fires during his 1907–11 term than the fireboat named in his honor ever put out—probably starting with his 1908 wedding to Josephine Lee, the only black first lady in Chicago history, who spent her last days in an Uptown convalescent home. "Ours was not a popular marriage," Mrs. Busse confided to journalist/playwright Ben Hecht shortly after her husband's death in 1914.

Although no official mention was ever made of her color, the nuptials were conducted in virtual secrecy. A short time later, the new Mrs. Busse filled out amended birth certificates listing her brother and two sisters as white. Yet according to Hecht, Josephine Lee Busse referred to the then-popular black singer Dido Delong as her niece on more than one occasion.

And a longtime friend recalled years later that "she was so light complected she passed for white." Fred himself didn't know she was black until just before he married her. Even his brother George said at the wedding that "Fred could get himself in dutch oftener than any wise bird on earth."

The Republican bon vivant, who made a fortune in the coal and hardware business before serving in the legislature, then became Illinois treasurer and Chicago postmaster on his way to the mayor's office. Those who knew him swore he would never give anything less than a half dollar for a shoeshine. Yet he had so badly dissipated his assets that by the time he died, his widow ended up with only fifteen cents.

In 1916—two years after Fred Busse's death—a sympathetic city council made the destitute widow collector of hopeless debts, an act of charity that turned out to be one of the best moves ever made by any Chicago politician. By 1935, she had brought in at least $3 million the city had previously written off as uncollectable. "I never sent any persuasive letters. I just told them to pay up or else," Mrs. Busse once explained.

Her career abruptly ended in 1946 when she broke her hip and lay on her hotel room floor for two days before anyone found her. She spent the rest of her life in hospitals and nursing homes, dying at the Bethany Methodist Home, 5050 North Paulina, in 1961 at eighty-three.

Blacks Had Their Own Hideaway on a North Side that Needed Them, Provided They Stayed Invisible

Back when blacks were a rarity on the North Side, they were more than welcome on the 4600 block of North Winthrop. In fact, they had to live there. The Central Uptown Chicago Association spent $14,000 in 1940 to get a city law spelling it all out without equivocation: "No Negro person can buy, own or rent property in this district except on that block [the 4600 block of Winthrop] which is inhabited entirely by Negroes."

First to live on that almost-hidden stretch of Winthrop between Leland and Wilson, Jacki Lydon notes in her *Legends and Landmarks of Uptown*, was "a black chauffeur whose employer left him a home on the block in his will." Judson Jenkins, one of the Chicago Police Department's first black detectives, and "Rollins Lambert, the first black priest ordained by the [Catholic] Archdiocese of Chicago, also lived there for awhile."

In those days, the only reason blacks were even allowed to live on that one segregated block was as "the help" in the homes and apartments of the upper-middle-class whites or to work in the restaurants and shops serving their needs, community organizer Iberus Hacker told a reporter in the 1970s. Over the years, "railroad porters, department store clerks and domestics created a place of their own, held block parties, watched each other's children, gathered on summer nights for outdoor movies, fought in two world wars and did an honest day's work for an honest day's pay," noted Lorraine Swanson in the online *Lake Effect News.*

Back in the day, Collier's Famous Chicken on the southeast corner of Winthrop and Leland was owned by one of the original Winthrop families and widely considered the best fried chicken restaurant in the city.

"It was the kind of place where if you were a kid who did something on one end of the block, somebody—most likely your parents—would know about it before you reached the other end," a longtime resident remembered.

Many of the early black families—descendants of slaves—migrated here from Arkansas, Mississippi, Tennessee and Alabama, according to Earline Clark, matriarch of the Winthrop Avenue family. Clark said some, including her own grandparents, "came to Winthrop Avenue because it was the only block in Uptown that would rent to African American families."

"There must have been some kind of underground communication among black folks that said, 'Hey, y'all come on up to Winthrop,'" Emmanuel

Lewis told Swanson. "We continued to stick together. There was no violence. Everybody looked out for each other," said Lewis, who grew up on the 4600 block during the 1950s.

Tonia Lorenz said she didn't know about the block's black history when she bought a condo in one of the new buildings and "spent a lot of time filling dumpsters with weeds and trash from the vacant lot across the street." But all things considered, Lorenz added she had nothing much to complain about. After all, she told Swanson, "The Winthrop Avenue pioneers had to deal with something far uglier than a weedy lot. They had to deal with enforced legal segregation, but they didn't let it stand in their way."

Looking back, however, "For the generations of McKeevers, Browns, Clarks, Jenkins, Thurmans, Austins, Grays, Lewises, Joneses, Colliers and Bakers that grew up there, most thought it was just a place where their folks wanted to live," said Swanson, who covered a 2009 dedication of what became the Winthrop Avenue Family Historical Garden on a once-neglected vacant lot.

A special plot in front of the lot will be kept by descendants of the original Winthrop families who will grow flowers and vegetables, with a dozen more plots used by community groups.

"This is the first block of Winthrop. This is where the street starts and keeps going north. It's kind of ironic that this first block was inhabited by the most decent, dignified, classy black folks I've ever been around in my life," Emmanuel Lewis said.

Uptown Was Never the Same in Wake of World War II and a Changing Economy

Some blamed Uptown's decline at least partly on the World War II housing shortage that compelled the breakup of many spacious homes into rooming houses where—as in Edgewater—the wives of servicemen at Great Lakes Naval Station and Fort Sheridan found inexpensive housing. The postwar years saw a flood of impoverished southern migrants into the rooming houses and residential hotels. Others said the decision to extend the outer drive not only helped kill the Edgewater Beach Hotel but also cut off the once-chic Wilson Avenue and Sheridan Road shopping strips from easy access.

Postcard of the Edgewater Beach Hotel Opera Company performing *Faust* on a platform on Lake Michigan. Date unknown.

The Peter Kranz house at 5896 North Ridge.

By the mid-1950s, Uptown had already developed a reputation as "Hillbilly Heaven" as well as a port of entry for American Indians who left the reservations looking for nonexistent jobs after the federal government cast large numbers of Indians adrift on their own. Bars with names like the Teepee and the Reservation soon cropped up all over Uptown. Fortunately, so did the American Indian Center (AIC), 1630 West Wilson. Opened in 1953, the AIC is now the country's longest continuously operating urban Indian service center, serving members of some forty tribes from all over the country, not just the nearby Menominee, Sac, Fox and Potawatomi who migrated to the North Woods after being driven out by white settlers in the early nineteenth century. The AIC has hosted nearly twenty different social service organizations and, at last report, even sponsors a Sea Scout troop that meets on the SS *Red Cloud* in nearby Montrose Harbor.

On 9/11, the AIC held an American Indian religious service—complete with drums and chants—blending the traditions of the different tribes represented at the center. "Don't forget, we're Americans too," one of the Indians told a reporter at the end of the drumming ceremony that evening.

In 1963, the Council of the Southern Mountains opened the Chicago Southern Center with the help of local philanthropist and insurance mogul W. Clement Stone, author of several motivational books on PMA (Positive Mental Attitude). Stone, a self-made millionaire who lived to be nearly one hundred, worked to the very end of his life to help people and groups of all descriptions pull themselves up by their bootstraps—with a little help from a friend.

Others argue that it didn't help when the state turned Uptown into an open-air psychiatric ward. According to the late Loyola University sociologist Ed Marciniak, about seven thousand "deinstitutionalized" patients were released to Uptown halfway houses in one year alone. To make matters worse, many of these patients relapsed because they no longer had anyone to make sure they took their medication.

In his report for the Uptown Chicago Commission in the early 1960s, Jack Meltzer noted that 600 of Uptown's 2,800 residential buildings had been broken up into rooming houses and about one-fifth (260) of all the stores in the community were taverns, "some with notorious reputations."

By the 1970s, Uptown had fallen far from its place in the stars as a haven for the rich and chic during the Roaring Twenties and even during the Depression, when Al Capone held court at the Green Mill, 4802 North Broadway. At one point, a 25 percent stake was given to St.

Valentine's Day mastermind "Machine Gun" Jack McGurn to persuade comedian Joe E. Lewis not to jump ship to the New Rendezvouz at Clark and Diversey.

But if Joe E. Lewis was the joker, Mary Louise "Texas" Guinan was the Green Mill's Queen of Hearts. A study in contrasts, the Waco, Texas–born hurricane attended a convent school before moving with her family to Denver, where she performed in amateur theater productions and played the organ in church. Mary Louise married a newspaper cartoonist, moved to Chicago, broke into vaudeville, ran the Green Mill and even found time to deliver lectures at places like the ballroom of the Illinois Women's Athletic Club, where she gave the lowdown on "Why Husbands Stay Out Nights." The by-then thrice-divorced entertainer reminded her audience that "men are like children and need to be treated like children. If they want to play boss, let them play boss. What do you care? You know you have the edge on them."

The cops shut down the Green Mill after a shooting incident involving the club's manager and a business associate. The acclaimed "High Priestess of Whoopee" moved on to New York as a chorus girl and proprietor of a fashionable speakeasy frequented by celebrities, including columnist Walter Winchell. Winchell just happened to have written the script for one of Guinan's early movies, *Broadway Through a Keyhole*, in which she played a speakeasy proprietress. Years later, Winchell said Guinan was the one who introduced him to the Broadway scene, which over the years became so much a part of his gossip column career. But it didn't stop there. Talent scouts as well as the in-crowd of the time frequented her New York club and discovered two of her dancers, future film stars George Raft and Ruby Keeler.

By then, the New York police had also discovered the place, but the increasingly frequent prohibition raids didn't faze Guinan, who was reportedly raking in $700,000 in ten months from her various interests. Back in those days, the bill for a few glasses of hooch and a show in one of her establishments could run $100.

Opposite, top: Clement Stone, multimillionaire "Power of Positive Thinking" exponent, chats with an unidentified woman during a community meeting in the 1980s.

Opposite, bottom: Trumbull School back in 1910.

When she died at forty-nine in 1933 while performing in Vancouver, British Columbia, 7,500 mourners turned out for her funeral. Among the pallbearers were bandleader Paul Whiteman, writer Heywood Broun and two of her ex-lawyers. Her parents donated a tabernacle to St. Patrick's Church in Vancouver in thanks to the pastor, who was with the Ultimate Party Girl during her last hours.

All the way through the '50s, the quickly reopened Mill continued to play to a packed house with swing and jazz, drawing crowds from the nearby Aragon Ballroom and the Riviera and Uptown Theaters between shows. But by the mid-'70s, business started going down the tubes. In 1986, Dave Jemilo made one of his boyhood dreams come true by buying the club and bringing back the old décor, ambience and musical fare. Jazz remains a staple, featuring noted talents like Patricia Barber, a weekly regular for more than fifteen years, as well as emerging talents like the magnetic Melodie Magnuson on open-mic nights.

Today's Green Mill hosts a weekly Poetry Slam emceed by a local poet, Marc Smith, who also does a traveling show, *Sandberg to Smith—Smith to Sandberg*, where he combines the works of both poets with jazz music.

Originally opened in 1907, Pop Morse's Roadhouse, as the Mill was then known, was a favorite hangout for silent silver screen stars from the nearby Essanay Studio. The owner even put in a hitching post for "Broncho Billy" Anderson and other celluloid cowboys like William S. Hart and Wallace Beery, who would ride their horses over to Pop Morse's.

The Green Mill got its name from the Chamales brothers, who put a large green windmill on the roof as Chicago's answer to Paris's legendary Moulin Rouge ("Red Mill") and then introduced outdoor dancing and a rumba room. The rest of the block reportedly evolved around the Mill.

Tom Chamales, one of the Mill's early owners, built the Riviera Theater a few doors down the block.

Legend has it there were (or are) secret tunnels that Al Capone had installed under the Green Mill that led to the Aragon Ballroom, 1108 West Lawrence. Another of a cluster of faux Moorish entertainment palaces making up what urban planners envisioned as a revived entertainment district, the Aragon was an immediate success the moment it opened in 1936 and remained a major attraction through the 1940s. Over eighteen thousand people often turned up in any given week, undoubtedly with the help of the elevated trains that practically stopped across the street. WGN radio, then as now a major station in a major market, broadcast the music of Frank Sinatra, Guy Lombardo, Lawrence Welk, Wayne King and Duke

Ellington for an hour from the Aragon every night to audiences across the Midwest and parts of Canada.

The forty-six-thousand-square-foot Uptown Theater at 4816 North Broadway, also with an Iberian-inspired interior, opened with 4,381 seats, making it the largest cinema in the United States at that time, including New York's Radio City Music Hall. And it looks it, with an eight-story façade and five-story entrance lobby.

Its grand opening on August 18, 1925, featured a parade of more than two hundred floats and a grand ball at Harmon's Arcadia, 4444 North Broadway. An estimated 12,000 people waited in line for tickets to the first show. According to some accounts, several women collapsed from exhaustion. Back then, the Uptown had a staff of 130, including uniformed ushers and a full-time, fourteen-piece orchestra, a nurse and even firemen. While other theaters had the usual vaudeville acts, intermission stage shows at the Uptown would follow the movie's theme.

While the crowds dwindled in the late 1960s and early 1970s, even when the Uptown started running triple features, the theater resurrected as a major concert house in the 1970s but has been closed since 1981 when a frozen water pipe burst, flooding much of the interior. Since then, the Uptown has been used for location shots for movies such as *Backdraft*, *I Love Trouble* and *Home Alone 2*.

In 2006, restoration work began, and some of the terra-cotta pieces were stored for future use. JAM productions—which also owns the Riviera Theater a block north—bought the Uptown for $3.2 million in 2008. The Friends of the Uptown Theater, including founding member Andy Pierce; former 48th Ward alderman Mary Ann Smith; and Rick Rabiella, whose father once owned the theater, have appeared in a documentary on the hard times faced by historic buildings all over the United States. The fight continues, not only to save the best of the clubs like the Aragon and movie palaces like the Uptown and Riviera but also the big, elegant hotels like the twelve-story Sheridan Plaza, another Spanish Revival treasure built in 1925 still standing at Wilson and Sheridan; the Grasmere at 4621 North Sheridan; and the Chelsea, 920 West Wilson, that soon sprang up around the entertainment district.

Not far away from the Uptown nightlife area was the 5100 (Broadway) Club, where Danny Thomas was discovered by "Uncle" Abe Lastfogel, head of the Morris Talent Agency. Lastfogel launched Thomas on a spectacular career that included the starring role in *Make Room for Daddy*, which ran from 1953 to 1964. While still a struggling comic, Thomas—a devout Catholic—

had made a promise to God that if he ever became a success, he'd build a shrine to St. Jude Thaddeus, patron saint of impossible cases. Good as his word and then some, Thomas founded St. Jude Children's Hospital in Memphis, Tennessee.

Edgewater

Once One Community, Uptown and Edgewater Drifted along Their Very Separate Ways

While Edgewater was riding high making movies and living it up along the lakefront, Uptown just to the south was swinging at places like the Green Mill, the Aragon Ballroom and the 5100 Club—thanks at least partly to the 1900 opening of the Northwestern Elevated Railroad's terminal near Wilson and Broadway (now part of the Chicago Transit Authority's Red Line). The current station was built in 1923 to accommodate both the el trains and the North Shore suburban commuter line. Some shops and a repair yard were added but destroyed in the mid-'90s fire that triggered a years-long, often bitter battle between yuppies and low-income residents backed by populist alderman Helen Shiller over whether to put in upscale housing and retail outlets or some kind of subsidized housing for poor families and senior citizens.

An Aldi supermarket, a Target store and mixed-income housing eventually went in. Sensing the direction the demographics were turning, Shiller decided not to run in the 2011 election, ending twenty-four years in the city council that often pitted Uptown's haves and have-nots against one another.

It was a battle that had been simmering since the mid-1960s, when plans were announced to build a city college on almost a square mile of low-cost housing in the middle of Uptown. Groups like JOIN (Jobs or Income

Above: Bryn Mawr Avenue, 1920s.

Opposite, top: A dairy cart makes its rounds.

Now), led by Rennie Davis—later to make headlines as one of the "Chicago Seven" defendants charged with inciting riot during the 1968 Democratic Convention—demanded greater economic opportunities. At the same time, Reverend Iberus Hacker's Rainbow Coalition and Chuck Geary's Uptown People's Planning Coalition called for a moratorium on redevelopment or at least creation of a low-income Hank Williams Village developed with public and nonprofit foundation funds. As far as possible, they also wanted the project designed and built by black, Appalachian and Hispanic tradesmen and architects.

To nobody's surprise, "the first Mayor Daley, Richard J.," as one longtime resident put it, got his way, and Truman College opened in 1976. Today, the two-year school has nearly thirteen thousand students, many of them the very people Hacker, Geary and others fought so hard for.

Truman College has attracted its share of world-class visitors, including former Polish president and Nobel Prize recipient Lech Walesa, who in May 1995 picked the school's auditorium to make a historic plea that his country be admitted to NATO. After all, Poland's first post-communist leader said, Chicagoans can play a crucial role in shaping the future of the world—and he wished Chicagoans would start soon.

The Gdansk shipyard worker who helped topple the Soviet monolith when he said he was fed up and wasn't going to take it anymore told a standing-room audience to think of him less as a world figure than as "your Uncle Lech who's come to talk with you for awhile."

Walesa warned that despite the collapse of the Soviet empire and the end of the Cold War, threats to Poland's independence had not disappeared. He also discussed the then-impending Russian elections, in which Russian voters ultimately decided to stick with the sometimes oafish president Boris Yeltsin rather than return to a form of Communism.

But he seemed less worried about former Communists returning to power in his own country, explaining the alternatives would have been even worse. "I had a choice between being another Castro or letting democracy run its course," said Walesa, who was himself driven from office by voters unhappy with the transition from Communism to a Western-style economy that triggered inflation, unemployment and crime. Like it or not, to interfere would have negated everything his Solidarity movement had worked for, Walesa said.

Ironically, Walesa did not participate in the Gdansk shipyard strike that propelled him to world prominence, said Truman College teacher George Otto, who helped get Walesa to the Uptown campus. Otto said the government and the strikers gave workers like Walesa the opportunity to leave the shipyard before the strike began. Walesa left but soon returned after realizing his place was with the strikers, leaping over the locked gates to rejoin them.

Walesa also proved he hadn't strayed too far from his roots as a shipyard electrician. When the microphone started squeaking and college officials began squirming, Walesa himself ran from the podium to adjust the speaker wires. "See, no problem," he laughed.

There Was More to Edgewater's "Secession" than Met the Eye, Local Historians Say

Like most "divorces," the Edgewater Historical Society's Robert Remer and LeRoy Blommaert point out, the real reasons for Edgewater's 1980 split from Uptown wasn't as simple as homeowners on the affluent end of a neighborhood wanting nothing to do with the "low-lifes around Wilson and Broadway" who were "giving the whole neighborhood a bad name," as a 1999 *Chicago Reader* story suggested. The real reason Edgewaterites lobbied for their own community was that they believed they deserved one "based on the historical record," said Blommaert in a letter to the *Reader*.

A Delightful Drive Through Lincoln Park

TO EDGEWATER On the Lake Shore.

$5,100 TO $10,500

New modern detached houses, on lots 50x 150 feet.
One to four blocks from Lake Michigan.
A strictly residence suburb with high-class improvements.
Absolutely the most desirable and cheapest residence property in Chicago.
Terms to suit you.
Splendid building lots, $40 to $80 per foot.

42 daily trains and 7-cent fare by the C., M. & St. P. R. R. The Chicago and Edgewater Electric Car Line will be running June 1.

Salesmen leaving city office every day at 9, 9:30, 10:45, and 12 a. m., or 2:30 and 3:30 p. m., will take you free of expense to inspect the property.

For terms, plans of houses, etc., apply to

J. L. COCHRAN, 722 Chicago Opera House.

A RESIDENT AGENT AT EDGEWAT

An ad promoting life in Edgewater helped bring hundreds of middle-class residents to J.L. Cochran's lakefront community.

The Edgewater Coal Company making a delivery at the Kranz Home. Coal was the main fuel in the days before gas heating.

An early J.L. Cochran real estate office. The pioneer developer took every opportunity to promote Edgewater, including persuading a commuter rail line to build stations in Edgewater. He later regretted making the area too accessible to lower-income residents.

A look inside the McManus grocery store.

Blommaert said Edgewater had always been considered a separate community both by the Edgewater Community Council and even the area's founder, John Lewis Cochran, who came up with the name back in the 1880s. Uptown, Blommaert said, got its name around 1915—thirty years later—from Loren Miller's Uptown Department Store on Broadway between Lawrence and Wilson.

"While statisticians and city planners did not recognize Edgewater as a separate community, its residents did. When the city finally gave Edgewater recognition as a distinct Chicago community, the action was viewed by Edgewaterites not as secession from Uptown but the correction of an error made many years earlier by a University of Chicago sociologist without any residential input.

"Since Edgewater never joined Uptown in the first place, it could not secede from it," Blommaert said.

EL TRAINS WOULD HAVE MADE FOUNDING FATHER JOHN COCHRAN TURN OVER IN HIS GRAVE

While Edgewater was first settled by a handful of Swedish and Luxembourger cabbage and celery truck farmers, the community itself arguably sprang from the brow of John Lewis Cochran. The pioneer developer started buying lakefront land around 1886, first to build mansions for the well-heeled and then to build more modest housing a few blocks west.

After dubbing his subdivision "Edgewater" for obvious reasons, Cochran put in sidewalks and streetlamps, founded the Edgewater Light Company and persuaded the Chicago, Milwaukee and Saint Paul Railroad to add a stop at Bryn Mawr, then helped set up the Northwestern Elevated Railroad to run all the way to Howard Street. The Father of Edgewater would have considered all that one of his few big mistakes.

After all, the easy commute attracted doctors, lawyers, junior executives—the yuppies of their day—and created canyons of apartment buildings along Kenmore and Winthrop that would become the near-slums of the late 1950s and 1960s. During World War II and its aftermath, the once-luxurious apartments were broken up into studios and one-bedrooms, first to serve war workers and then the overflow from neighboring Uptown of destitute transients, low-income retirees and assorted unfortunates.

By 1960, the Kenmore/Winthrop corridors had become such a blight that local residents created the Edgewater Community Council (ECC), which by the late 1970s was working with groups like the Organization of the Northeast to get a freeze on any new halfway houses. Edgewater, like Uptown to the south, was being inundated with waves of mental patients being released from traditional state-run mental hospitals. Most came from nearby Dunning, officially known as the Chicago State Hospital, where practically all but the worst cases were released, provided they promised to stay on their meds. Few did.

By 1974, there were some 6,150 apartments in just the eight blocks from 5600 to 6400 North Sheridan Road, making that strip one of the most densely populated places in the entire city. By then, the ECC was pressing the city to separate Edgewater from Uptown on its official map of recognized neighborhoods. The council got its wish in 1980 when the city granted the divorce, designating Edgewater as Community Area 77.

J.L. Cochran, founder of Edgewater.

All the while, local activists like the late Charlie Soo were hard at work promoting Argyle between Broadway and Sheridan as "Chinatown North," while a large slice of Andersonville had morphed into an unofficial gay and lesbian enclave.

Even Locals Found Edgewater Beach a Dream Getaway

The *tres tropicana* building at 5555 North Sheridan looks like it would have been perfectly at home in Edgewater's halcyon days.

It was.

The Edgewater apartments were the home of luminaries ranging from controversial Chicago public school superintendent Ben Willis to Chicago Bears founder George Halas, a prim-and-proper sort who got the building's management to ensure decorum by enforcing a rule keeping women in shorts from parading through the lobby. The "help" was also barred from passing through any of the "public areas" whether they were on duty or not, recalled one longtime resident. Fortunately, things lightened up over the years in the "Pink Building," as it is still fondly called. Even the newsletter is still titled *In the Pink*—and printed on pink paper, of course.

Not surprisingly, people often confused the apartment building with the hotel itself. Both were matching buildings designed by Benjamin Marshall. The hotel opened as a four-hundred-room operation in 1916 costing $9 million, and the apartment building was added a dozen years later. That three-hundred-unit "Pink Building" underwent a more than $14 million renovation in 1999. As in days gone by, it still features amenities like a sixty-foot heated indoor pool and adjacent party space, exercise rooms, a library, a craft room, two acres of gardens, a shopping arcade, a floral/gift shop, a two-level indoor garage and bike rooms and an in-house restaurant.

From 1916 to 1967, the other half of the matched set, the Edgewater Beach Hotel (EBH), 5349 North Sheridan, was a home away from home to everyone from FDR, Ike and Mahatma Gandhi to Arabia's King Saud and the Sultan of Swat himself, Babe Ruth. Visitors also included Marilyn Monroe, Frank Sinatra, Judy Garland, Bette Davis, Tallulah Bankhead and Nat King Cole. On hand were the big bands of Benny Goodman, Tommy Dorsey, Glenn Miller, Artie Shaw and Wayne King, who were also heard on the hotel's own radio station, WEBH, a forerunner to WGN.

And where else on Chicago's North Side could you find 1,200 feet of private beach and a lighted tennis court that could be converted into a skating rink in winter? Here, performers including Xavier Cugat and Abbe Lane (and later Charo), camels and dancing elephants entertained in the legendary Marine Room and on an outdoor terrace opening to a dining room with a sliding skylight.

While it wasn't cheap, prices are always relative. A menu from the early 1920s offered whole baby lobster for $1.50, smoked salmon for $0.60 and a cold roast beef dinner for $1.25. You weren't paying for the food as much as the ambiance.

But as always, life wasn't as glamorous for everyone, several members of the Dorothy Hill Dancers recalled in a story by Adam Langer in the November 9, 1989 *Chicago Reader*. The wages and benefits weren't bad for the times (dancers got $30 a month plus room and board and could order anything they wanted off the menu). If they lived at home, they got $40. "But it was like a reformatory. You had to go straight to your room," one-time line captain Ruth Homeguth told Langer.

"Dorothy Hill was very unpopular, but she got results," conceded Alice Ann Knepp, another dancer.

Like any major hotel, the Edgewater Beach had its moments. Like when a honeymooning couple racked up a $1,568.02 bill (back when that was real money) before finally confessing they were broke.

Or former organist Betty Gray's recollections of the guy who was literally dying to dance with one of the women at his ringside table. "This one gentleman who was just recovering from a massive heart attack mentioned to one of the guests that he would like her to dance with him around the floor. Just around the floor for a little bit over to the organist because he wanted to ask me for a request or something.

"She said, 'You are just getting over a heart attack. You should not be dancing.' He said, 'I'm gonna do it.' They danced from there across the floor, and he dropped dead right in front of the organ."

Then there was Xavier Cugat, who Ms. Gray said was "always exciting because whenever he was [at the EBH], he had trouble with the ladies. They crashed down the door. And Abbe Lane appeared nude here…

"The funny thing was that Abbe Lane, who was much younger [than Cugat], had all those sharp-looking, sometimes Latin, very sexy men come up to dance with her, and Cugat, being [thirty-three years] older, always got those matronly, heavy women. And it just floored him. He did it for a few weeks and then he quit [doing it] because he was horrified at the type of women he drew. He thought he'd get girls like Abbe Lane and he didn't."

Or when nineteen-year-old Ruth Steinhagen shot former Chicago Cubs star Eddie Waitkus back in June 1949 in a bizarre scenario that became the inspiration for part of the novel and movie *The Natural*. Although they'd never met, it seems Steinhagen had a major crush on Waitkus, who'd been traded from the Cubs to the Philadelphia Phillies two years before and was in town to play against his old team. So the insurance company typist did what any girl might do under the circumstances. She took her life savings, bought a .22 rifle, checked into the Edgewater Beach and gave a bellboy five dollars to take a note to Waitkus inviting him to her room.

She ordered two whiskey sours and a daiquiri from room service and waited. He called around 11:00 p.m. Assuming she was the usual baseball groupie, he went straight to room 1297-A at her invitation. She opened the door, said she had a surprise for Waitkus and—true to her word—whipped out the gun and fired one bullet, piercing a lung and lodging in Waitkus's back.

Steinhagen called the hotel operator, said she had just shot someone and then knelt beside Waitkus and held his hand as they waited for help to arrive. Steinhagen said she'd planned to kill herself after shooting Waitkus but lost her nerve at the last minute.

Although recovery required several operations, Waitkus was able to resume his baseball career, playing six more seasons and even the 1950 World Series when the Phillies played the New York Yankees. The Phillies lost.

Steinhagen was charged with attempted murder but was declared insane and committed to an asylum for three years. After the shooting, police found an "altar" to Waitkus in her room at 1950 North Lincoln Avenue.

"I had my first good look at him [Waitkus] in 1947. I used to go to all the ball games just to watch him. We used to wait for them to come out of the club house after the game. And all the time I was watching him, I was building in my mind the idea of killing him. I knew I would never get to know him in a normal way, so I just kept thinking, I will never have him, and if I can't have him, nobody else can...I didn't know how or when, but I knew I would kill him," she wrote in an autobiographical sketch after the shooting on instructions from her court-appointed psychiatrist.

Because Waitkus declined to press charges, she became a free woman, living the rest of her life as a virtual recluse until her death in June 2013 at age eighty-three.

Some Lakeside Trade Shows Were Truly to Die For...

As with many top-tier hotels, the Edgewater had its share of memorable trade shows—like when a national morticians' association made "Make the World a Better Place to Die" the theme of its October 4, 1927 convention. Speakers at the upscale undertakers' meeting called for brightly colored caskets and "cheerful" business attire instead of the then common black frock coats. The image-conscious group also called for the elimination of black-plumed hearses and the custom of decorating door knobs with black crepe.

While Arthur Mann of Knoxville, Tennessee, described the perfect mortician as both "cheerful and optimistic," he criticized colleagues who took to playing golf, "leaving a slovenly assistant to run the business." After all, Mann said, "a mortician of high character has little time for the lighter sports."

Of course, by the end of the convention, Mann's colleagues passed a resolution that they all start referring to themselves as funeral directors instead of morticians or undertakers and that the word "coffin" be replaced by the supposedly less somber-sounding "casket." Chicagoan Jack Matthews, the group's executive director, went even a step further, arguing that "a casket of rose has no less dignity than one of brown or gray." Rose-colored coffins "suggest that the dead is living in the beauty and fragrance of flowers," he said, predicting that "in the next few years, the color of caskets will run the gamut of the rainbow, the symbol of hope that God himself set in the sky."

...But in the End, the Venerable Old EBH Itself Expired on Christmas Eve

The Edgewater Beach Hotel may well hold the record for one of the longest, most complicated strikes in labor history. From 1934 to 1939, representatives of twenty-two different unions picketed outside. By the time it was all over, neither labor nor management was sure who had started the trouble.

During the Depression, the EBH was one of the few hotels that stayed in the black. By the late 1950s, however, the hotel was on a slow but steady decline. Some say it was because the northern extension of Lake Shore Drive cut the beach off from what was by then a one-thousand-room complex. Others blamed the downturn on a shift in emphasis from the "carriage trade" to the convention business. Others recall it was because the stucco walls were so thick they couldn't install central air conditioning. Still others claim people stayed away because the place had become too "mobbed up" for comfort. Al Capone was a frequent guest who reportedly held business meetings at the hotel.

Either way, the hotel's owners filed for bankruptcy in late 1967, claiming they were losing $1,100 every day the place stayed open.

At 9:00 a.m. on December 21, a lawyer abruptly fired the two-hundred-member staff and gave the sixty-five permanent residents until 5:00 p.m. to move out. Many found emergency refuge in other North Side hotels like the Belmont, Webster, Drake and Belden-Stratford. Some old-timers got a few days' reprieve, but the management still turned off the heat to keep them from delaying their departures too long.

Judge Thomas Courtney, who had lived there for thirty-four years, demanded an investigation by State's Attorney Edward Hanrahan, adding that "if Bolshevism has anything on this, I'd like to know what it is."

The very last guest, nightclub singer Lima Kim, finally checked out on Christmas Eve.

Edgewater Has Seen Its Share of Things that Go Bump in the Night

Back in the 1990s, Jim Soens and some fellow Civil War reenactors were standing by the front gate of Rosehill Cemetery one midnight when a woefully over-served vagrant freaked out. "What are you guys doing up at this hour?" he asked Soens.

Soens smiled, explaining, "We've been buried here for about 130 years, so every now and then they let us get up and walk around."

According to Soens, the drunk turned white and hightailed it down Western Avenue.

"He probably never touched another drop after that," Soens mused, still chuckling over the prank.

But while the nameless inebriate only thought he was seeing ghosts, there have been other spectral visitations in Rosehill and nearby that may have been anything but pranks. Although *Chicago Haunts* author Ursula Bielski says Rosehill prohibits its employees from talking about what she describes as some of the graveyard's "more active residents," there are a few of what she describes as "particularly spirited sites."

Like the Hopkinson Mausoleum, whose occupant began moaning and rattling chains when the owners of some nearby plots took the cemetery and Hopkinson family to court, complaining that the finished tomb would overshadow their grave site. The case went all the way to the Illinois Supreme Court, which ruled that the complainants should have known something like that could happen. The mausoleum's construction resumed, but Bielski says people still hear faint moans and rattling chains on the anniversary of Charles Hopkinson's death.

Not far from Hopkinson's tomb, a cemetery employee reportedly saw a woman in a long gown seeming to float above the ground. Bielski said that when the groundskeeper approached the lady, she "dissolved into a

Stewart Dawes and Lorraine Holmgren cut the rug during a Valentine's Day 1987 senior dance.

mist." The next day, a woman phoned the cemetery office claiming that her deceased aunt had appeared to her the night before, complaining she had not been "properly remembered" with a tombstone after her death. When Rosehill workers went out to check the lot, they found the unmarked grave was at the same place where the previous night's apparition had occurred. Once the stone was in place, Bielski said, nobody ever saw the woman again. It appears she just wanted to be remembered. And she has been, Bielski said.

Still other apparitions have reportedly occurred at the grave of twenty-year-old Frances Pearce Stone and her infant daughter who died in 1854. The grieving husband and father commissioned glass-encased likenesses of his loved ones, said Bielski, noting that on the anniversaries of their deaths, a white haze seems to fill the glass case and the statues of mother and daughter seem to rise to greet their visitors.

But wait, it gets better, said Bielski, noting that even Rosehill's most famous permanent residents aren't necessarily guaranteed eternal rest. Mail-order pioneer Aaron Montgomery Ward reportedly walks the halls of Rosehill's elegant condo-mausoleum hoping to get a rise out of one-time rival Richard

Sears of Sears Roebuck & Co. Bielski says cemetery workers tell her it hasn't happened yet.

And the hauntings don't stop at Rosehill's gates, she said, noting otherworldly goings-on at the nearby St. Andrew's Inn, 5938 North Broadway, where spirits have been high for years. According to Bielski, the previous owners, Jane McDougal and her son Blair, began noticing flying glasses and allegations of drinks being drunk by unseen imbibers back when the bar was known as the Edinburgh Castle Pub. The prime suspect, as far as the regulars are concerned, is Frank Giff, long-deceased owner of the tavern at that address back in 1964 when Giff, a heavy drinker, would often fall asleep in a stupor after closing time. Another theory is that Giff hit his head after falling from a bar stool. Either way, Giff was in for a very long sleep interrupted only when his spirit would gulp down the paying patrons' drinks or when he wasn't rubbing some girl's back or knee, Bielski said.

Sands and Tides Brought Tropicana Flavor to Edgewater during Nifty Fifties

Not surprisingly, the EBH and the "Pink Building" attracted three surfside motels that brought their own unique taste of Miami Beach to the Edgewater lakefront during the 1950s through the mid-'60s.

First came the Sands on the northeast corner of Sheridan and Foster in 1955 following a 1953 zoning change lifting a ban on motels within the city limits. The Sands, advertised as only eight minutes from the Loop, featured a pool, cabana and 150 air-conditioned rooms. The Sands was soon followed by the 52-room Tropicana (later the Lakeside Motel) at 5440 North Sheridan and the 200-room Tides at 5223 North Sheridan.

As rising land values made it financially impractical to put relatively small motels on relatively large parcels, the Tides and the Sands were razed in the 1970s and replaced with a Dominick's supermarket. Since its demolition in 2005, the Tropicana is now an empty lot. Still another local motel, the one-hundred-room Holiday Lodge at 4800 North Marine, later became a Salvation Army shelter.

According to Patrick Steffes in the Forgotten Chicago blog, Edgewater was once home to 30 percent of these urban motels designed to serve business and trade-show visitors. "Motels were looked at as being more modern than some of the established [downtown] hotels and therefore a more preferable place to stay," Steffes noted during an Edgewater Historical Association talk.

The motel concept started with construction of the U.S. Interstate Highways back in the 1930s, Steffes said. As people began driving farther from home, they found little lodging outside downtown areas, he added.

SOVEREIGN ALSO RULED AS HOME TO VISITING KINGPINS

Just down the street was another celebrity hangout, although nowhere near as elegant as the Edgewater Beach. Nevertheless, the EBH got some competition from the Edgewater Athletic Club in the Sovereign Hotel, 1040 West Granville, where Chicago's own Johnny (Tarzan) Weissmuller was a lifeguard during his high school years.

Guests not only included Al Capone, the Andrews Sisters and Charlie Chaplin but also King Christian X of Denmark and England's Duke of Windsor. According to unconfirmed but persistent rumors, the Prince of Wales, the future King Edward VIII of England, may have had an affair during his visit that resulted in an illegitimate child. The then Prince of Wales reportedly met the lady during a party at the Saddle and Cycle Club. In any case, a North Side faucet maker wasn't above running an ad trumpeting how "The Prince of Wales stopped here and liked Chicago Faucets.

"Of course he didn't say so. One doesn't mention that sort of thing, you know. But just let Chief Engineer Henry Luhr of the Sovereign Hotel tell you why he likes Chicago Faucets…"

STILL NO SOLID LEADS IN THE 1935 MIDNIGHT MURDER AT THE SADDLE AND CYCLE CLUB

Opened in 1895 as an oasis of exclusivity in the heart of what was already the playground of the rich and famous, the Saddle and Cycle Club at 900 West Foster was started as a way station for cycling enthusiasts on what were then adventurous day trips into the country. According to an 1899 *Chicago Tribune* story, fashionable architect Jarvis Hunt and two fellow bikers "felt the necessity of having some place where they and their friends might be able to rest after a spin without being obliged to patronize the public gardens."

Four years after the club opened, Hunt designed a sumptuous clubhouse complete with a veranda overlooking a pool, stables, boathouse, pier and a three-hole golf course—all about one hundred feet from the lake's original shoreline.

Chicago's upper crust who could afford the dues rushed to join, at least partly because of its seclusion. It took a six-hour bike ride or an hour and a half on horseback to get from downtown or the North Shore. For a hefty ten dollars (which included champagne), members' wives and children could also make the trip from the Deerpath Inn in Lake Forest, which made a stop at the Saddle and Cycle en route to the city.

But being who they were, the Saddle and Cycle's members soon set up their own stagecoach line, "The Blue Dog," named for the water taxi that brought visitors up the lake from the Loop. According to Jacki Leyden and Chet Jakus in their 1980 book, *Landmarks and Legends of Uptown*, the lake route "was certainly the most elegant way to arrive at the Saddle, and picnic baskets and games supplemented the good times on board. Once ashore at the Saddle, clambakes on the beach were followed by dancing under the stars."

In 1907, the Saddle and Cycle built Chicago's first swimming pool, complete with statuary and a formal garden along the pool's edge.

But what's now the nation's only country club in the heart of a major city was the scene of a still-unsolved murder they probably don't talk about much. Early on February 3, 1935, Louis Straub, forty-six, the Saddle and Cycle's night bartender, was shot seven times with a .38-caliber pistol and then left to die in a basement washroom.

When Straub's wife, Helen, arrived around 2:00 a.m. to pick up her husband, he was nowhere to be found. By then worried Straub may have fallen ill, she got help from the night watchman, who found her husband's bullet-riddled body. Although Straub's wallet was empty, his watch was left behind and there were no signs anyone tried to force open the safe.

Police theorized Straub was apparently waiting outside when he met his killer, probably someone he knew since he wouldn't have let a stranger inside at that hour.

A taxi driver told police he picked up a woman he later said looked a lot like Ellen Edin, identified as a close friend of Mrs. Straub, and drove her to the Saddle and Cycle Club at about the estimated time of the murder. The cabbie told police the woman had him wait for her. About fifteen minutes later, the woman bolted out of the clubhouse, jumped in the cab and ordered him to "get the hell out of here" and take her to a bar on Argyle Street, not far from where the Straubs lived. Employees said the woman bought a bottle of whiskey and left but told police they were sure the apparently thirsty lady wasn't Mrs. Straub.

Still, there was at least some reason to suspect the grieving widow, who told police and the *Atlanta Constitution* that "Louis was the best husband in the world" and that she didn't know of any other women in his life. "We were very happy." But it didn't take the cops too long to learn the Straubs' marriage wasn't exactly made in heaven.

The club's night watchman, Gus Schwartz, told police and the press that Straub often brought women to the club's bar after closing time. Police at one point told reporters that "it was easy to discern that as a husband he may have left something to be desired."

Helen Straub, on the other hand, may have found comfort in the arms of several women in her bridge circle, especially Ellen Edin, who had received a $150 watch from Mrs. Straub. According to the *Tribune*, "it was no secret among the [bridge players] that Straub and his wife had been on the verge of a break since last summer over Mrs. Straub's affection for Mrs. Edin." The *Tribune* suggested that "this strange tangle of life and loves...probably deserves the attention of a neurologist as well as a policeman."

Detectives also learned of a $10,000 insurance policy on Louis Straub's life naming Mrs. Straub as sole beneficiary, with a double indemnity—$20,000—in case of violent death. Never explained was how the Straubs were able to live in a luxury apartment well beyond the reach of any bartender—even one working two jobs.

Interestingly, Mrs. Straub told police she had bought a pistol from her father several months before her husband's murder and later sold it to a former paramour, Peter Breckie. Mrs. Straub at one point revealed during questioning that Breckie "threatened to kill Louis so that he and I could be together." Breckie confessed engaging in "improprieties" with Helen Straub but denied wanting Straub dead or buying the .38 from Mrs. Straub. His story that he was nowhere near the Saddle and Cycle Club the night of the murder was corroborated by his wife.

In 1936, during a legal battle over whether Helen Straub should finally get the $20,000 life insurance payout, attorneys representing Louis Straub's brother Ernest—arguing that Helen Straub herself killed her husband—brought in fifty witnesses, including a neighbor who testified seeing Mrs. Straub slash her husband with a butcher knife and on another occasion hit him in the head with a flowerpot. A night clerk at a hotel where Louis Straub sometimes lived recalled Straub telling him he had survived an earlier middle-of-the-night shooting attempt at the Saddle and Cycle Club in 1926. The judge, however, ruled there was no conclusive evidence linking Mrs. Straub to her husband's murder and awarded her the $20,000.

One final note: Three years after that trial, Kenneth Colling, the taxi driver who drove the mystery woman to the Saddle and Cycle the night of Straub's murder, was arrested for helping arrange a robbery.

To this day, the Louis Straub murder—an incident the Saddle and Cycle would probably prefer to forget—remains unsolved.

DID HEIRENS KILL SUZANNE DEGNAN? FOR SOME WHO REMEMBER, THE JURY IS STILL OUT

The March 2012 death of William Heirens, whose sixty-five years behind bars made him reputedly the longest-serving prisoner in the United States, if not the world, rekindled debate over whether Heirens actually committed the crime that shocked a generation of North Siders—the January 6, 1946 murder and dismemberment of seven-year-old Suzanne Degnan, a student at nearby Sacred Heart Academy.

The police investigation into a disappearance or possible abduction turned into a high-profile manhunt when Suzanne Degnan's severed head—still wearing a blue ribbon in her hair—was found in a sewer behind the 5800 block of North Kenmore Avenue. As the day went on, body parts were found in several places along Kenmore Avenue. The little girl's arms weren't found until after the funeral at St. Gertrude's Church attended by some 1,300 mourners.

One way or another, this wasn't the kind of crime that was going to be allowed to end up in a cold case file.

Police were quick to arrest Hector Verburgh, a sixty-five-year-old janitor, about a block away from where the Degnans lived. "This is the man," officers said after forty-eight hours of questioning and torture and then released Verburgh without charges after a lawyer for the janitors' union got a writ for his release.

But there were other leads that turned cold. Mayor Edmund Kelly received an anonymous note "to let you know how sorry I am not to get ole [*sic*] Degnan instead of his girl. Roosevelt and the OPA [Office of Price Administration] made their own laws."

The house at 5943 North Kenmore where Suzanne Degnan was murdered by William Heirens in one of the North Side's most sickening crimes.

Because a meatpackers' strike was underway and Suzanne Degnan's father, James, was a senior Midwest official of the OPA, which at the time was considering extending wartime rationing and price and wage freezes, police briefly entertained the possibility that the note writer—and Suzanne Degnan's killer—might be a meatpacker. By April, about 370 suspects had been questioned and released before Heirens was arrested for trying to burglarize an apartment building at 1320 West Farwell. Police said Heirens's fingerprints matched those found in the Degnan home and on a note sent right after Suzanne Degnan's disappearance demanding $20,000.

After being given sodium pentothal and questioned for six days without his lawyer present, Heirens confessed to the Degnan murder as well as those of Josephine Ross, 4109 North Kenmore, and Frances Brown, 3941 North Pine Grove, where someone had scrawled in lipstick, "For heaven's sake, catch me before I kill more. I cannot control myself." Heirens confessed, later claiming he did so only on the advice of his

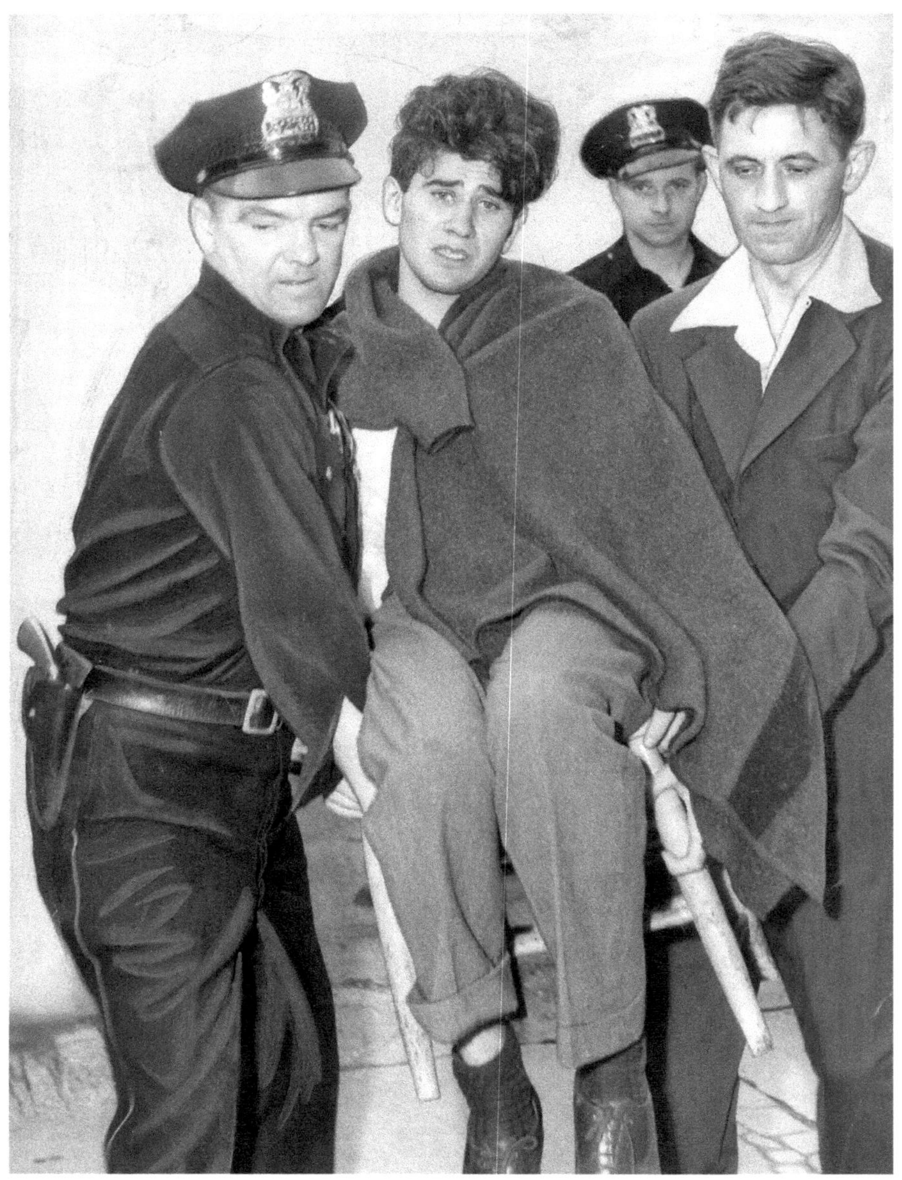

Officer John Keane and Detective John Ashcher carry Heirens into a hospital in a chair. *Chicago Sun* photo.

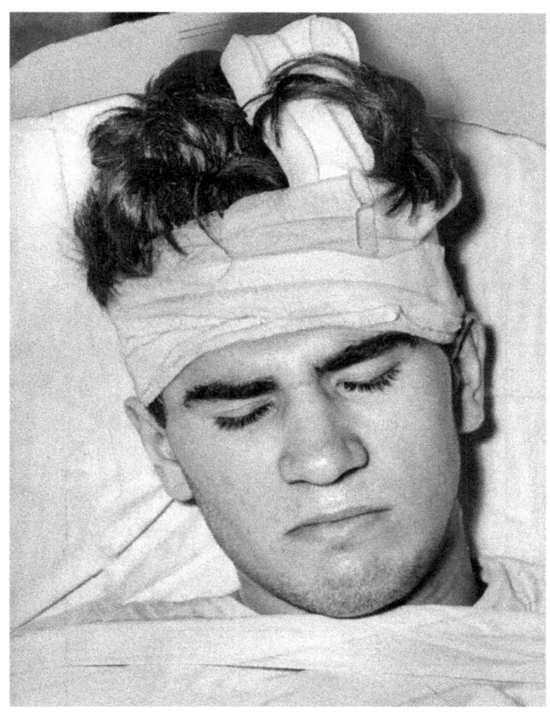

Child killer William Heirens with bandaged head, in what police described as a "phony" coma.

lawyer and family to avoid the death penalty. His claims of innocence convinced Dolores Kennedy of the Northwestern University Center for Wrongful Convictions, who considered the fingerprints and other evidence dubious at best.

On the other hand, according to the late longtime Lerner Newspapers executive Richard Bjorklund, former Chicago police commissioner Timothy O'Connor, who had worked the Degnan case, said he had no doubt that whoever killed Suzanne Degnan also killed the other two women. There were probably only one or two men in Chicago who would have left behind the evidence police found at the scene, O'Connor reportedly told Bjorklund. The killer left a calling card—defecation—at or near all three crime scenes, O'Connor told Bjorklund.

But as time went on, a growing number of skeptics began questioning whether the bookish model prisoner Heirens had become could have committed such crimes. While at Stateville Prison, Heirens became the first prisoner in Illinois history to earn a four-year college degree behind bars and went on to take a wide range of courses in several languages, data processing, analytical geometry and tailoring. For five years, Heirens was manager of the prison's uniform factory, where he supervised 350 inmates.

After being moved to the lower-security Vienna prison, Heirens set up a prisoner education system and took still more classes. But prison officials drew the line at courses in physics, chemistry or celestial navigation. Heirens was clearly too smart for them to take any chances.

Not surprisingly, the family of Suzanne Degnan was just as determined to keep Heirens behind bars. Betty Degnan Finn, who was ten years old when her sister was murdered, and brother Jim Degnan remained steadfast, attending every one of Heirens's parole hearings for nearly thirty years. Even if Heirens had been drugged and beaten during lengthy interrogations, Jim Degnan told the *Chicago Sun-Times*, "it still doesn't change the fact that he did it."

When a federal appeals court ruled in 1983 that Illinois inmates convicted before 1973 couldn't be denied parole on deterrence grounds and magistrate Gerald Cohn ordered Heirens's immediate release, Illinois attorney general Neil Hartigan vowed to fight the ruling. "Only God and Heirens knows how many women he murdered. Now a bleeding heart do-gooder decides he's rehabilitated and should go free. I'm going to make sure this kill-crazed animal stays right where he is," Hartigan said.

The Illinois General Assembly passed an advisory resolution opposing Heirens's release, and Hartigan's office was ultimately able to get the federal appeals ruling overturned.

The Illinois Prisoner Review Board remained unconvinced Heirens was ready for release in 2007, despite failing health and an exemplary prison record. "God will forgive you, but the state won't," parole board member Thomas Jones told Heirens at the end of that last hearing.

"Babbling Burglar" Helped Separate Cops from Crooks; Police Force Was Never the Same

It's hard to believe a casual conversation over a set of "nice golf clubs" would have led to the nastiest scandal—and the biggest changes—in the history of the Chicago Police Department. But that's exactly what happened one evening in June 1958 when Officer Frank Faraci stopped career crook Richard Morrison outside a liquor store at Berwyn and Broadway asking to be cut in on his burglary jobs.

During the testimony Morrison later gave in return for having all charges against him dropped, Morrison said Faraci told him some of the other Summerdale cops would also "go along with the show." As far as he was concerned, Faraci thought a set of golf clubs might be "nice" for starters.

"After all, we like nice things too," Faraci reportedly told Morrison, who was already well known to at least some of the Summerdale officers. Some knew him back in Swift Elementary School and later Senn High and met him again when he worked at Wesley's Pizza underneath the Bryn Mawr elevated stop when he delivered late-night snacks at no charge.

The deal was soon sealed. Morrison would break into the most promising businesses and homes while the cops acted as lookouts and helped cart away the loot, usually appliances, television sets, even shotguns. Then they'd meet at one of the policemen's homes and divvy up the loot. Morrison got cash while the others got the goods, which they in turn either kept for themselves or fenced to family and friends.

Soon it was the cops themselves who were deciding what places to hit. It was an especially useful arrangement, said Morrison, recalling the time he accidentally set off an alarm while trying to break into a tire store. Morrison's partners in crime were able to convince the cops responding to the alarm that they already had the situation under control. Another close call came during a music store break-in when Morrison's cops got him out the back door just as the other police were coming in the front.

If a job didn't look profitable enough once Morrison and company got inside, they just moved on to the next house or business on their list, said Morrison, recalling how they once did three burglaries in one night. Morrison, who claimed to be the "greatest burglar in Chicago history," once estimated he did 150 jobs in six months, netting about $100,000 worth of stolen goods.

As thieves go, he was probably sharper than average. Back in his teens and early twenties, he learned the safecracking trade by visiting security shops posing as a safe and vault buyer, asking about the location of tumblers, the thickness of steel and the strengths and weaknesses of various types of strong boxes. He'd buy top-quality manila ropes in ten-thousand-foot lengths and then make ladders to help him get into roof ventilation shafts and down through skylights. He'd never use the same equipment twice, even leaving his other burglary tools at the scene as if to dare the cops to "catch him if they can."

During his hours of testimony, he said uniformed police worked with him in at least ten major business burglaries in the Edgewater/Rogers Park/

Evanston area. Among them were the Edmond J. Self Custom Furniture store at 6322 North Broadway and the Western Tire & Auto Store, 5100 North Broadway, one-time home of the 5100 Club, where entertainer Danny Thomas got his big break a decade earlier.

It got to the point where the cops were not only helping Morrison and his sometime accomplice Robert Crilly carry the stolen items out to the squad cars but were also getting wish lists and filling those orders.

But it all ended on July 30, 1959—almost a year to the day after the cop/crook partnership started—when Morrison was finally arrested outside his apartment building at 4332 North Sacramento. According to Richard Lindberg, Morrison panicked and pulled a gun but was quickly disarmed. The detectives wanted Morrison alive and talkative.

After first clamming up, hoping his police buddies would help him out, Morrison began singing a different tune when he realized he was on his own. The "Babbling Burglar," as he was soon being called in the papers, turned state's evidence in return for immunity from prosecution—and the better accommodations, food and safety in the witness suites in the county jail. There, he was able to receive a steady stream of visitors, one of whom once smuggled a bottle of whiskey in a cake.

As soon as he started giving names, police were rousting the burglar cops out of bed at 1:00 a.m. and searching their homes. According to Lindberg, "It wasn't pretty."

During the raid on Faraci's house, a *Chicago Tribune* reporter saw the livid missus rip some baubles off her neck, screaming, "Here, you might as well have this too. I got it from Richard Morrison."

By morning, four truckloads of stolen goodies were recovered at seven of the eight officers' homes. The cops found nothing at the eighth officer's place.

But all eight were convicted in August 1961. Five were sentenced to one- to five-year prison terms. Two more were fined $500 each. And the one officer who had none of the stolen loot at his house got a $1,000 fine and six months in jail.

Before the trial was even over, the Chicago Police Department underwent the biggest changes in its history. Mayor Richard Daley almost immediately removed Commander Timothy O'Connor and created a five-man committee headed by Orlando W. Wilson, a California criminology professor who recommended himself. "Professor" Wilson got the job even though his only real experience—in Wichita, Kansas, and as a deskbound provost marshal during World War II—was years in the past. But he did shake things up.

For starters, he moved his office from city hall to police headquarters and reconfigured police districts so their boundaries were no longer identical to city aldermanic wards. He increased hiring of black officers, updated the record-keeping and communications systems and tightened discipline, even cracking down on officers taking free coffee or meals at local restaurants. But while Wilson was a virtual apostle of preventive patrol and rapid response, he eliminated most foot beats.

Despite these and other much-touted reforms, crime in general and homicides in particular skyrocketed. The murder rate went from 10.3 per 100,000 in 1960 to 24.0 per 100,000 by 1970. Morrison himself survived a murder attempt outside the criminal court building at Twenty-sixth and California on March 30, 1963. After his release from the hospital, Morrison moved to Fort Lauderdale, where he reportedly worked for a while as a police photographer.

As far as anyone knows, nobody in Chicago has seen or heard from Richard Morrison in more than thirty years.

Cop Killer Gus Amadeo Gunned Down after Watching Movie, Just Like Dillinger Twenty Years Earlier

Bank robber John Dillinger was led to his death at the hands of lawmen by a "woman in red" (actually, Anna Sage was wearing a deep orange dress that night) after catching a movie at the Biograph Theater in 1934. So was fugitive cop killer Agustino (Gus) Amadeo, also set up by a girlfriend in an orange dress after a movie on October 29, 1954, this time at Berwyn and Clark, at the end of a major manhunt by more than two hundred police officers.

This time it wasn't J. Edgar Hoover's G-men but a team of Chicago cops led by Lieutenant Frank Pape, described by *Return to the Scene of the Crime* author Richard Lindberg as "one of the department's most feared gunslingers" who was at one point on a short list to become Chicago's police commissioner.

Everything went ballistic, so to speak, when robbery detectives Charles Annerino and William Murphy were making the rounds, rousting lowlifes in the local dives when they found Amadeo in the Circle Lounge, 1756 West Lawrence. Amadeo had just escaped from the county jail and wasn't about

Local historian Morey Matson points to the machine gun bullet holes left from a 1930 drive-by shooting outside an apartment building at 5301 North Ashland likely intended as a "message" to North Side rackets boss George "Bugs" Moran on the first anniversary of the St. Valentine's Day Massacre, an incident many crime experts have always believed was intended to eliminate Moran. *Photo by Patrick Butler.*

to go back. During a brief struggle with the two detectives, Murphy grabbed for Amadeo's gun, which went off, hitting Annerino in the chest.

Amadeo managed to break free, and over the next few hours, Pape's men scoured the North Side, finding Amadeo's jacket by a Northwestern Railroad viaduct but no trace of Amadeo himself. Knowing Amadeo had occasionally dated Dolores Del Genio Marcus, sister of a West Side restaurant owner Pape knew had some recent troubles with the police, Pape installed a bug inside the eatery and soon learned Amadeo was hiding out on the North Side and needed a car. Though reluctant to cooperate at first, Dolores Marcus changed her mind after Pape reminded her about her brother's police problems. Sensible girl that she was, Dolores agreed to meet with Amadeus. Pape set the trap, but Amadeo never showed up.

The rendezvous was rescheduled for the next night when Amadeo planned to catch a movie at the Calo Theater, 5404 North Clark.

According to Lindberg, Amadeo was to meet Dolores in her car, which would be parked near Swanson's Drug Store at Berwyn and Clark at 7:30 p.m.

A small army three times the size of the detail that bagged Dillinger was hidden in unmarked cars, panel trucks, taxicabs and second-floor apartments up and down Clark Street. Other officers sauntered along the street disguised as day laborers and cabbies.

On spotting his quarry, Pape yelled, "Gus, stop right there." When Amadeo realized what was happening, he turned and ran across the street and then fired twice before being laid low by a shower of gunfire.

A bystander was also hit in the side but was virtually ignored by hundreds of gawkers, some dipping handkerchiefs into Amadeo's blood much as those who watched Dillinger die did a generation earlier.

Pape was promoted to captain five years later, and while he never really kept score, he's believed to have killed at least nine of the bad guys, sent five more to the electric chair and put another three hundred in prison during his storied career. Over his forty-plus years on the force, Pape estimated he was involved in at least sixteen shootouts. Family and close friends said the devout cop never went on duty without a rosary in his pocket. Pape was the subject of forty-nine stories in detective magazines and, according to Lindberg, was the inspiration for Lieutenant Frank Ballinger in the 1950s *M-Squad* TV series.

About the only thing anyone ever remembered about twenty-six-year-old Gus Amadeo was that he always seemed to be causing trouble.

Fed-Up Housewives Had It, Gave Machine the Boot

By the mid-1970s, political independents and community leaders like Lakewood/Balmoral activists Marion Volini and Marge Britton—already disgusted with crooked elections, ghost voters, saloon payoffs and vote buying in transient hotels—were having a morning kaffeeklatch discussing a series of unexplained halfway house fires when Volini suggested that Britton run for the aldermanic seat soon to be vacated by Marilou Hedlund. Britton suggested Volini run instead, since she had one fewer child than Britton to look after.

"We already had a tradition of community politics through our block club," Britton said.

Volini ran and lost to Dennis Block, a local lawyer who later ran as a Republican mayoral candidate and then moved to the suburbs, never to be heard from again. With Block out, Volini gave it another try, winning a special election in 1973 and then two full terms.

But as long as Martin Tuchow remained as Democratic ward committeeman, progressives and reformers considered a complete cleanup impossible. Volini backed independent Arnold Levy, who came close to winning a rough-and-tumble election in which several Tuchow precinct workers were arrested and convicted of election fraud.

Even more serious crimes came to light in 1983, when Tuchow and 36th Ward Democratic committeeman Louis Farina were convicted of conspiring to extort $7,000 from contractors who wanted city permits to renovate an Edgewater apartment building. Farina got four years, and Tuchow got eight. A year later, federal judge John Grady cut a year off Farina's sentence but said Tuchow—who had continued to practice law even after he was convicted and disbarred—deserved no mercy. According to news accounts of the hearing, Tuchow bawled like a baby.

Grady was unmoved. "Here he is in court [practicing law] after he had his license revoked by the Supreme Court of the State of Illinois. And he knew it was suspended," Grady said.

Tuchow ended up doing slightly over two and a half years on an eight-year sentence. After his release, he made several unsuccessful attempts to recover his license. He died at eighty-eight in retirement in Fort Lauderdale.

Before Tuchow's conviction, however, Volini supporter Robert Remer was picked by community residents to run against Tuchow's last-minute replacement in the 1984 election. Remer won and was credited by supporters with "returning the ward to the community," helping pave the way for the election of future committeemen, including Kathy Osterman, Marion Volini's son Michael and state senator Carol Ronan.

Volini gave the ward a thorough housecleaning before turning the job over to Bronx-born Kathy Osterman, who in 1987 ran first in an eleven-person primary race. The one-time Lawrence House social director broke into politics as a block club president before becoming then–State's Attorney Richard M. Daley's community relations director.

Two years later, Osterman resigned to head the Mayor's Office of Special Events, clearing the way for Daley to appoint one of her campaign workers, Mary Ann Smith, who served five terms.

Some longtime residents nodded approval when Smith carried on the ward's new tradition of "community politics" and gave the nod to

Osterman's son, Harry, who became alderman in 2011 after service as a state legislator.

Move Over, Bridgeport! Edgewater/Uptown Was Also an Incubator of Chicago Mayors and Wannabes

When Dennis Block jumped into his Quixotic long-shot 1977 race, he wasn't the first ambitious local politician with an eye on the fifth floor. Three, in fact, made it all the way.

Edward Fitzsimmons Dunne was the only man ever to serve as Chicago mayor and Illinois governor and then go on to a judgeship. He also found time to become a prosperous businessman and represent the American Commission on Irish Independence at the 1919 Paris Peace Conference at Versailles to lobby for a free Irish nation. He raised money for Irish Feinian rebels and then gave out of his own pocket and frequently hosted Irish statesmen, exiles and rebels in his Uptown home, which was also open to President Teddy Roosevelt, who stopped for lunch during a 1908 Chicago visit.

After serving from 1892 to 1905 as a circuit court judge, Dunne made a successful run for mayor and soon cut the cost of gasoline in Chicago from one dollar to eighty-five cents a gallon and slashed water bills from ten cents to seven cents per thousand gallons. Almost half a century ahead of his time, Dunne promised to bring in public ownership of public utilities.

After failing to win another two-year term because of his inability to deliver on that promise, Dunne went back to practicing law and in 1912 went to the governor's mansion, where he pushed for women's suffrage, prison reforms and a major infrastructure rebuilding program; organized a Public Utility Commission; and expanded the state's role in regulating workman's compensation and public schoolteachers' pensions.

After leaving office, Dunne helped create a National Unity Council to fight the Ku Klux Klan, which in the early 1920s was starting to make major inroads in a number of northern states.

William Dever may be almost forgotten today, but you can thank him for finishing Wacker Drive. Born in Massachusetts during the Civil War, he was lured to Chicago in 1887 by an ad offering jobs for leather tanners at twenty-five dollars a week. Three years later, he finished night classes at the Chicago College of Law and started attending discussion groups at the Chicago Commons settlement house on Milwaukee Avenue, where founder Graham Taylor persuaded Dever to run for alderman. Dever won on his second try. By 1910, he had become a judge, moving first to a new apartment at 708 West Buena in the heart of then-fashionable Uptown and later to an Edgewater three-flat he bought at 5901 North Kenmore.

Persuaded by Clarence Darrow that "Chicago needs a mayor who has the courage to say no, and say it to all his best friends," Dever ran in 1923 after Belmont Harbor's own William Hale (Big Bill) Thompson decided not to go for another term. During his two-year term, Dever appointed DePaul Law School dean Francis X. Busch his corporation counsel, made reformer Mary McDowell Chicago's welfare commissioner and picked Chief Morgan Collins to clean up the police department and enforce Prohibition. Dever even fought for public ownership of mass transit twenty years ahead of its time but in the end was sacked by the voters for shutting down hundreds of breweries and speakeasies.

Though personally "wet," Dever reminded groups like the Chicago Bar Association, "It's the law. What can I do but enforce it?" With Dever out of the picture, Thompson won the 1927 election, promising, "We'll not only reopen all the places these people have closed, but we'll open 10,000 more."

Dever became president of the Bank of America and campaigned to have mayoral terms expended from two to four years, explaining that "any man faithfully performing the duties of the office must be prepared to serve only a single term."

Another Edgewater mayor, Bridgeport-born Martin Kennelly, lived at the Edgewater Beach Apartments and was the founder of Allied Van Lines, a trade association that brought several cartage companies under a single management agency. When the Democratic machine bosses decided to can incumbent Edward Kelly, they turned to Kennelly as a "reform" candidate.

Like Dever, Kennelly was never your typical Democratic politician, which virtually guaranteed his undoing back at the height of the big city "machine" era. Despite his vigorous campaign as a "reform" candidate promising a major cleanup after the corrupt cronyism of Boss Kelly, the Democratic Party slate makers made one big mistake: they failed to take him at his word. The strait-laced civic crusader who ran for mayor from an apartment in the Bridgeport neighborhood where he grew up soon proved too independent and reform-minded for the political kingmakers.

In 1948, he made waves in some circles when he backed city censors who banned Jean-Paul Sarte's play *The Respectful Prostitute.* Regardless of how respectful the title character may have been, Kennelly refused an invitation by the producers to a private showing, explaining, "I do not like the play. I do not like the title. The title alone should be enough to ban the show as far as I'm concerned."

Still, the two terms of "Fartin' Martin" or "Marty the Mover," depending on your point of view, gave Chicago the Congress expressway and bridge, the Chicago Skyway and the start of the Northwest Expressway, the South Lake Shore Drive, the extension of the West Side subway and the start of O'Hare Airport.

Like Kelly, Kennelly was summarily dumped in 1955 by the regular Democratic committeemen and replaced on the ticket with fellow Bridgeporter Richard J. Daley, who went on to become the longest-serving—and most powerful—mayor in Chicago history.

Forced into retirement, Kennelly returned to what he did best—busying himself with community affairs—serving as president of Lincoln Park Zoo and the American Red Cross's Chicago chapter.

Early Streetcar Barns, Vintage Wilson Elevated Station Changed with the Times but Still with Us

Edgewater's first streetcar barn may be a little worse for wear, but the 1895 building constructed for the Chicago and North Shore Street Railway Company—the North Side's first trolley line—is still there at 5837 North Broadway, just south of the armory. Until sometime in the 1980s, a copper cornice emblazoned with the name of the Chicago and North Shore Street Railway was the only sign of the building's original use.

Not surprisingly, the car line's president and chief promoter was Edgewater founder John Cochran. According to the Edgewater Historical Society, it ran from central Evanston south on Clark Street, east on Devon and south again on Evanston Avenue (now Clark Street) to Graceland Avenue (today's Irving Park), where passengers switched to horse cars and later to the cable line at Dewey Court, just south of Clark and Diversey, for the final leg of the trip downtown. According to the EHS, the "Ardmore Barn," as it was known back then, was phased out in the early 1900s by a new car barn at 6330 North Clark that also still stands, at last report as an auto body shop.

A few miles south, it took about sixty years for the Wilson Avenue elevated stop to go from pristine to putrid—just like the surrounding neighborhood. Originally dubbed Uptown Station, local merchants and real estate developers had high hopes when what was to be the north terminal of the Northwestern Elevated Railroad—and the Wilson Avenue elevated station—opened in May 1900 with a waiting room, offices and shops across the street, between Wilson and Montrose.

At one point, Frank Lloyd Wright was brought in to design an entrance to the station but walked out on the job to go to Europe with Mamah Cheney, the wife of a client, after being all but run out of Oak Park by scandalized neighbors. Mrs. Cheney died several years later when a Barbados-born house servant set fire to Wright's Wisconsin home and then hacked to death Mrs. Cheney, her two children and two others who were staying at the house at the time.

The rapid transit line went bankrupt by 1916, when utilities mogul Samuel Insull created the Chicago Elevated Railways Collateral Trust, bought control of the failing line, elevated the ground-level tracks from Wilson to the city limits at Howard and built a new Wilson Avenue station while he was at it. The interior featured terrazzo flooring and marble paneling with a "grand staircase" leading up to a mezzanine-level ticket booth. Amenities included a ladies' restroom, smoking lounge and telephones. The basement area included men's facilities and a full-service barbershop.

The new station also handled baggage for the North Shore commuter line and even had a freight elevator from the ground floor to the platform, according to the Chicago Transit Authority, which took control of all elevated, streetcar and bus lines in 1947. Among the first things the new CTA did was to stop using Wilson Avenue as the end of the line for most trains and discontinue the practice of giving North Shore riders free transfers to the elevated trains.

But as the neighborhood changed, so did the station. Upscale shops slowly gave way to a pinball arcade and an assortment of fast-food joints. The barbershop closed, as did the washrooms, which by the late 1960s had become hangouts for drunks, dopers, thieves and perverts.

In 2012, the CTA unveiled a $200 million plan to renovate the ninety-year-old station—starting with restoration of the building's terra-cotta exterior and a redesign to allow what a CTA official described as "plenty of room for retail" on either side of the main entrance. Also planned are replacement of tracks and the viaduct over Wilson Avenue and the removal of support columns over nearby streets and sidewalks. The project is expected to be completed in thirty-three months.

When Tragedy Stopped at the Granville El Station

Until the 1977 Brown Line crash at Wabash and Lake that killed a dozen people and left 180 injured in the worst rapid transit disaster in Chicago history, that dubious distinction went to a November 24, 1934 collision at the Granville station. During the height of rush hour, a steel Wilmette-bound North Shore commuter train "telescoped" a wooden "Shoppers Special" elevated train, killing 10 and injuring 60, 36 of them seriously.

In an instant, wooden splinters flew and passengers hurtled to the street below. According to a *Chicago Tribune* story, Edward Price, who lived in an apartment at 6150 North Winthrop overlooking the el tracks, ran to the scene, called the fire department and began helping pull some of the victims to a nearby driveway. According to seventeen-year-old Joseph Iaclla, 1429 West Thome, who sold newspapers outside the Granville station, it took exactly four minutes for the fire engines to arrive and nine minutes for the first police ambulance to get there.

Cars and trucks were quickly pressed into service to take the injured to Edgewater, Swedish Covenant, Ravenswood, Rogers Park and St. Francis Hospitals. Police were posted at the entrances of these hospitals to control frantic crowds trying to push their way inside for news of their friends and loved ones.

Before long, an estimated five hundred police officers and twenty-five ambulances were on the scene. Three priests—Fathers J.J. Kieley and Thomas Doherty of nearby St. Gertrude's Church and Father Howard Ahern from DePaul University—administered last rites to those who appeared near death.

"We hardly felt the crash, but there was a tremendous noise. We saw a woman lying down near the third rail. Her skirt was burning. We pulled her away, beat out the flames and got her next to the station platform. Next we picked up two men. Both had been thrown across the tracks," said William Biesel, who had been riding the North Shore home to suburban Libertyville.

William Helm, an investment broker and longtime regular North Shore commuter, said the collision didn't surprise him. "I often thought the timing of the two trains was too close for safety," he told the *Tribune*.

The police and transit company officials wondered. Motorman Van Grooms, who was at the controls of the North Shore train at the time of the crash, was questioned for what seemed like hours by city, state and federal investigators. Two police officers waited at Grooms's hospital room to talk to the train's stunned driver. They never had the chance. Grooms's doctors said injuries and shock made it impossible for him to even testify in person at the inquest. According to Dr. C.T. McGarry, Grooms's injuries included severe lacerations of one leg and chest bruises.

Deputy Coroner James Whalen, who eventually obtained the only statement made by Grooms, said the shell-shocked motorman told him he was going about forty miles an hour behind the el train, which was supposed to pull over to a local track and let the North Shore train go by. "The lights on the el train were so dim I couldn't see them until I put on my brakes, but it was too late to stop," Grooms told Whalen.

Bernard Fallon, general manager of the Chicago Rapid Transit Co., ultimately blamed the accident on "human failure or the human element." Cook County state's attorney Thomas Courtney said he wouldn't hesitate to bring manslaughter charges against any elevated employees suspected of criminal negligence.

While investigators officially blamed Grooms for being too close to the el train and failing to stop in time to avoid a collision, Grooms was never charged with criminal negligence. In their report, however, the investigators urged an end to the practice of using steel and wooden cars on the same tracks and recommended the phasing out of the wooden cars as soon as possible—something that wasn't done until 1957. They also recommended installation of automatic signals along the tracks so the trains could keep their distance from one another—something that wasn't done on that part of the el system until the 1970s. It was too late to prevent another serious el/North Shore collision at the Wilson Avenue stop a few miles south of Granville twenty years later.

Like the Granville collision, the November 5, 1956 Wilson Avenue crash that resulted in eight deaths and about two hundred injuries was caused by putting trains from two different lines on the same track. Only this time, it was the el that slammed into a North Shore train instead of the other way around. Of course, it didn't help that the North Shore ran ten trains on that one track shared with the Chicago Transit Authority trains over a one-hour period. Shortly after 5:00 p.m., the North Shore's six-car Milwaukee Limited had just finished picking up and dropping off passengers when an eight-car CTA train doing fifteen miles an hour collided with the North Shore interurban. A coroner's jury ruled that the CTA motorman was to blame for the collision. Still a mystery is why the driver didn't see the North Shore train in daylight hours.

THE GRAND OLD ARMORY HAS BEEN MANY THINGS TO MANY PEOPLE OVER NEARLY A CENTURY

Probably the ultimate in recycling is the almost century-old Broadway Armory, 5917 North Broadway. Built in 1916 as the Winter Garden ice- and roller-skating rink, the block-long behemoth was taken over by the Illinois National Guard in the 1920s. Some longtime residents still remember seeing army trucks, Jeeps and even tanks and cannons rolling out of the huge doors on Broadway to training exercises at Fort McCoy, Wisconsin.

When the military no longer needed the facility some fifty years later and was considering selling it for commercial development, the Edgewater Community Council collected twenty-two thousand signatures urging that it instead be sold to the Chicago Park District for an indoor recreational

State Senator Art Berman, Sister Mary Woknicki of St. Gertrude's School, Kathy Osterman and George Coonley of the Chicago Department of Planning take part in a 1984 panel discussion on the future of the Broadway Armory. Osterman is credited by a number of longtime neighborhood residents with getting the city's foot in the door by encouraging the Park District to start renting space in the building even when the National Guard was still there.

Alderman Mary Ann Smith (48th) talks to an unidentified constituent during an Edgewater Community Council meeting at the Broadway Armory.

Broadway Armory employees stop for a group photo in April 1938.

center. "Save the Armory" rallies were held, attracting support from elected officials and concerned community residents.

The result was the city's largest indoor park, complete with a two-hundred-seat theater, soccer and volleyball courts and space for shuffleboard, line dancing, weightlifting, adult aerobics and ping-pong.

In a way, the military briefly returned to the old armory in 2011 when the National Theater of Scotland moved in with its award-winning performance of *Black Watch*, the saga of one of the UK's oldest regiments soldiering on in early twenty-first-century Iraq. And if you look carefully, you can still see faint patches of motor oil on the ground floor from the tanks and trucks.

Luxembourgers Immigrated en Masse to Edgewater, Gave Us the Area's First Undertaker

When Grand Duke Jean of Luxemburg visited Edgewater in 1984, nobody was particularly surprised. After all, most of the North Side's fifty to seventy thousand Luxemburg Americans are descended from the third of that country's population who immigrated here during the last half of the nineteenth century. Many started the truck farms along Ridge Avenue that eventually became the celery capital of the Midwest.

Among the first settlers was Nicholas Kranz, whose inn and farmhouse then known as the Seven Mile House near what is now Clark and Ridge was reportedly where presidential hopeful Abraham Lincoln attended an 1860 "farmers' caucus."

Luxembourger settlers beside Kranz included Nicholas Girsch, who ran a blacksmith shop near Rosehill Cemetery, and Heinrich Birren, a wagon maker and blacksmith who decided to put more life into his business by helping the bereaved take their grief out of their living rooms and into his newfangled "funeral parlors." One was located for years at 6125 North Clark Street.

Back in the mid-1800s, all you needed was a hearse, some carpentry skills and maybe a correspondence course in embalming. The business of prepping corpses for the next world had been growing in popularity since the Civil War, when traveling undertakers worked the battlefields preparing the remains of well-heeled soldiers for shipment back home at the family's expense. Birren, however, didn't have to wait for a war to see

Winandy's General Store, early 1900s.

that his future lay in the afterlife. After building an especially fancy hearse for what was then Chicago's only mortician, Birren decided to become an undertaker himself. One of his sons, Cornelius, eventually opened a funeral home of his own on North Avenue. Another opened Lake View's first mortuary on Lincoln Avenue.

Birren and his contemporaries had latched onto an idea whose time had come. By the early twentieth century, mortuary science was becoming a full-blown profession requiring formal schooling and state licensing. Today's laws, incidentally, bar the use of once-popular embalming chemicals like strychnine and mercury. It was becoming too hard to investigate suspected poisoning deaths.

Was the Old Engine 70 Firehouse Causing Firefighters' Cancer Deaths?

Other still-mysterious deaths are apparently linked to the old Engine 70 firehouse at 1545 West Rosemont. Back in 2000, Chicago Firefighters Union Local 2 began complaining that as many as thirteen fire department personnel assigned to Engine 70's quarters had developed cancer over the previous decade. The city ordered a study to determine whether environmental factors may have played a role and then ordered the station closed and replaced with a new house for Engine 70 a few blocks away at 6030 North Clark Street.

According to CFD spokeswoman Molly Sullivan, health issues were "not a factor." The 1906 firehouse was just too small, she said.

The replacement firehouse dedicated by Mayor Richard M. Daley eight years later was anything but. The $9 million one-story sixteen-thousand-square-foot "green" building had a silver LEED (Leadership in Energy and Environment Design) rating. The "bells and whistles" include twenty rooftop solar panels to heat water in the building, locker room and washroom facilities for today's male and female firefighters, a fully equipped gym, training areas for firemen and their officers who work round-the-clock shifts and a circular driveway to make it faster and safer for vehicles to get in and out of the new building, which houses not only Engine 70 but also Engine 59, which had previously been quartered at the 5714 North Ridge firehouse built in 1927.

Surprises of All Sorts Were Commonplace at St. Gert's, Even at Midnight Mass

Quick! Who doesn't belong on this list? Comedian/civil rights activist Dick Gregory; radio/TV personality (and possible future saint) Bishop Fulton J. Sheen; General William "Wild Bill" Donovan, head of the World War II Office of Strategic Services; Reverend Jesse Jackson; controversial Cook County state's attorney Ed Hanrahan; and Ernie O'Laughlin.

Everyone but O'Laughlin was a featured speaker at one time or another at "St. Gert's" current affairs forum. O'Laughlin was the guy who streaked midnight Mass at St. Gertrude's Church, 1420 West Granville, on one Christmas Eve in the early 1970s.

St. Gertrude's graduating class, circa 1915.

According to Chicago author, raconteur and *Irish News* columnist Mike Houlihan in his book *Hooliganism*, O'Laughlin became a living legend in some parish circles when some friends bet him fifty dollars he didn't have the nerve to streak Christmas services. Never one to back down from a dare, especially when he was fortified with plenty of Guinness, O'Laughlin "stripped down to his shoes, pulled a ski mask over his head…and got ready to step into history" just as the choir was crooning "O Holy Night," according to Houlihan's account gleaned from several "anonymous witnesses," who swore it was a stark naked O'Laughlin they saw bolt into the church, take a hard left in front of the main altar, fall on his keister in a half-assed genuflection and then dash out the exit before anyone could stop him.

Once outside, Houlihan said, a freezing O'Laughlin reportedly begged the Virgin Mary herself to "get me outta this and I will never, never, never come to church naked again."

Houlihan said that after hearing the story, he called St. Gertrude's rectory to get confirmation from then-pastor Father Bill Kenneally, who said that while he wasn't at the parish back then, anything's possible. After all, "St. Gertrude's has a long mythology," Father Kenneally told Houlihan.

And it always was a little ahead of its time, said parishioner Patrick Reardon, a *Tribune* reporter who wrote a book on St. Gertrude's first one hundred years. In 2008, Reardon noted, St. Gertrude's Growing in Faith committee began interdenominational discussions with several local non-Catholic religious communities, including the Emanuel (Jewish) Congregation, the Ismaili Center, Ebenezer Lutheran Church and North Shore Baptist.

Reardon also recalled how, in 1984, Father Kenneally started holding "reach out" Masses in the gym building for "those who were a little uneasy with Church, who are willing to give religion one more chance." The result, Reardon said, was an "informal...upbeat, jazz-influenced mass," which included a then–almost unheard of dialogue homily for "those on the edges of Catholicism."

While not all the old-timers were pleased, Riordan said, probably St. Gertrude's biggest controversy came on Pentecost Sunday 1988, when Kenneally proposed using part of the vacant convent to house six unwed mothers and their newborns. Opponents packed the meeting, arguing that "the building which had housed celibate sisters would be the home of sexually promiscuous women setting a bad example for the school children. Crime on the block would rise," Reardon recalled, summarizing the naysayers' arguments.

The plan was ultimately dropped, said Reardon. "While injured feelings lingered and scars remained, the issue fizzled out. The parish old-timers had been heard. The faith family at St. Gertrude's moved on."

"We did reach a level of at least civility and a certain amount of tolerance," Father Kenneally said. "Unlike many other Catholic parishes in Chicago, St. Gertrude's had never been identified with any single ethnic group," Reardon said. "Rather, it had been a religious family where over the course of a century people of diverse backgrounds, viewpoints and social status have searched together to understand the message of Jesus and carry it out."

Dawn Wyman, another longtime parishioner who opposed the plan to house single mothers in the old convent, agreed. Over the next two decades, she told Reardon, the parish "blossomed" under Father Kenneally.

Now considered one of the most vibrant, diverse parishes on the North Side, St. Gertrude's has come a long way since early 1912, when a handful of founding parishioners celebrated their first Mass in Father (later Monsignor) Peter Shrewbridge's apartment at 6320 North Magnolia. A few months later, 257 people met in the Hayt School Auditorium, netting $46.26 (the equivalent of $1,040 in today's money) in their first collection, Reardon said.

Parishioners soon moved to an unheated wood-frame, one-story church where it was often so cold in winter that Father Shrewbridge had to put his hands on the ceremonial cruets to thaw out the water and wine. But those early parishioners proved so unselfish that the materials for a new church were paid in full by the time the stock market crashed in late 1929. "The parish women even donated their wedding rings and other jewelry for a solid gold chalice with 30 diamonds," Reardon said, adding that the first chalice still exists, though rarely seen in public today.

Among the well-known parishioners at St. Gertrude's were Cook County state's attorney Dick Devine, sports columnist John Carmichael and personal injury lawyer Phil Corboy, remembered by classmate John Gaughan in Reardon's short history of the parish. "We were playing touch football [in the Hayt playground] when Phil Corboy, going out for a long pass, looked back over his shoulder for the ball and ran full smack into the baby slide with his arms outstretched," Gaughan recalled. "We took him to Clark Street, stopped a passing motorist and asked the man to take Phil to Edgewater Hospital. The game continued."

After all, Reardon said, "St. Gert's parishioners always seem to find a way to carry on."

How Greed Killed a Once-Great Community Hospital

Once counted among the city's leading medical facilities—complete with a rooftop helicopter landing pad and state-of-the art equipment including a hyperbaric oxygen pressure chamber used for treatment of gas gangrene, carbon monoxide poisoning, cerebral palsy and multiple sclerosis—Edgewater Hospital, 5700 North Ashland, was shuttered in disgrace in 2001.

"Practically everyone in the neighborhood was born at Edgewater," a longtime resident said—even Hillary Clinton and serial killer John Wayne Gacy.

For years there had been grumblings and murmurs about the way the hospital was being run during the long, some would say autocratic reign of Dr. Maurice Mazel, who founded Edgewater during the start of the Depression in 1929 and stayed at the helm until his death in 1980. But this was far different than just a matter of management style.

Investigators found some of the doctors there had been performing unnecessary surgery, even amputations, on homeless patients hanging around methadone clinics. According to testimony at the trials that followed, hospital employees would be sent out to recruit patients, sometimes even if they had no ailments or insurance. After giving these "patients" money, food or cigarettes, the recruiters reportedly coached these "patients" on how to fake certain symptoms to qualify for treatment, according to an American Urbex online feature. Doctors involved in the scheme would then bill Medicare and Medicaid and even some private insurance companies. According to court records, these insurers reimbursed Edgewater Hospital for more than 750 unnecessary operations performed by just one surgeon, Dr. Andrew Cubria.

Another doctor, Krishnaswami Siram, claimed he saw 187 patients—all with congestive heart failure—in just one day, November 12, 1997. And despite a severe snowstorm in January 1999, Dr. Siram reported visiting 31 homebound patients and another 18 in various medical facilities. Shockingly, 32 of Dr. Siram's patients were still racking up medical bills after they had died, according to one report.

When some of the patients started getting suspicious as they began seeing very hefty figures on their benefits explanation forms, they contacted the Wisconsin Physicians Service (WPS), which handles some claims in the Chicago area. The WPS, in turn, brought in the FBI. Soon, the hospital was spending over $1 million in legal costs trying to hold off a federal fraud lawsuit.

Dr. Siram was arrested, and the federal government, which had been paying 90 percent of the Edgewater Hospital's billings by that time, immediately halted all Medicare payments. The hospital shut down, and the fifty-two inpatients who were there at the time were transferred to other facilities.

By 2006, the courts slapped Peter Rogan, Edgewater's owner and CEO, with $64.2 million in damages and penalties. Rogan was then charged with perjury and obstruction of justice for trying to hide his assets in various Caribbean countries. Also convicted were senior vice-president Roger Ehmen and medical director Dr. Ravi Barnabas. Ehmen got six and a half years' prison time and was ordered to pay $5 million in restitution. Barnabas got four years and four months and had to pay $1.1 million restitution.

As of mid-2013, the hospital was shuttered and several community groups were still arguing over whether to put a park or a condo development on the site.

HILLARY CLINTON, CHICK EVANS, BURR TILLSTROM, "MOSES" AND THE LONE RANGER ALL WENT ON TO FAME

Easily the most famous Edgewater native is former U.S. first lady and former secretary of state Hillary Rodham Clinton, who was born in Edgewater Hospital and spent her first four years at 5722 North Winthrop. While the original house has long since been razed, an eight-unit condo building went up in its place: the Rodham Arms.

Her father, Hugh, ran for 49th Ward alderman in 1947 (back when the 49th Ward ran as far south as Bryn Mawr). He apparently did better in the manufacturing business than politics, coming in fifth with only 382 votes out of 26,071 cast. Democratic Ward committeeman Frank Keenan walked off with 17,073 votes (65.5 percent), with Republican Joseph Reubens coming in second with 5,509 votes. The Rodham family moved to suburban Park Ridge a short time later.

Another Edgewaterite who made good was Jack Carlton (Clayton) Moore, who played the Lone Ranger in four movie serials, five TV series, six feature-length films, novels, comic books and a comic strip over three decades, from the 1930s through the 1960s.

Born in his family's Queen Anne–style home at 6254 North Glenwood, Moore attended Hayt Grade School; Sullivan Junior High, where he was drum major; and Senn High School, where he was a gymnast. His first show business job was as an acrobat at the 1933 Chicago World's Fair at age eight, and at age nineteen, he left for modeling and acting jobs in New York. After World War II service in the U.S. Army Air Corps, where he made training films, Moore did publicity tie-ins with the Texas Rangers baseball team.

In 1978, he lost his trademark black mask when Jack Wrather, the owner of the Lone Ranger character, got a court order barring Moore from making any future appearances as the Lone Ranger. Wrather was planning a new film series with a different star and didn't want Moore making public appearances as the Lone Ranger. Moore put on different clothes and replaced the mask with a pair of black wraparound glasses, then filed his own successful suit against Wrather and continued his appearances until shortly before his death on December 28, 1999.

But Clayton Moore was only one of several notables to come from Edgewater. While attending Northwestern University, actor Charlton Heston lived and worked here. In fact, he told the *Chicago Tribune* in 1956,

Inside a blacksmith shop on Clark Street near Foster Avenue, early 1900s.

"All that I am—or almost all—I owe to the co-op apartment building at 5510 North Sheridan. When I was in college, I was the midnight to 8 a.m. elevator operator there. This gave me a good share of the night to read Shakespeare and the Old Testament. I read for voice and diction."

Another credit to Senn High School was Burr Tillstrom, creator of the *Kukla, Fran & Ollie* TV show, which ran from 1947 to 1957 as part of the Chicago School of locally produced, no-frills programs that included the Dave Garroway and Studs Terkel shows.

Tillstrom, a native North Sider, began work with a WPA-sponsored Chicago Park District puppet theater while still a University of Chicago freshman and in 1936 created *Kukla*, who got his name when a ballerina called him the Russian and Greek pet name for a doll. In 1939, Tillstrom's *Kuklapolitan Players* performed at the New York World's Fair.

The *Kukla, Fran & Ollie* show that evolved over the next few years is widely considered to be the first kids' show to appeal to both children and adults. The show's grown-up fans included two-time presidential candidate Adlai Stevenson, actor Orson Welles, authors John Steinbeck and James Thurber and actress Tallulah Bankhead.

In addition to the *KFO* show, Tillstrom appeared regularly on the *That Was the Week That Was* satirical revue. He won an Emmy for his "hand ballet" on that show depicting a couple separated by the then–recently built Berlin Wall. Once asked why he considered puppeteering so special, he explained, "You can express things that happen only in the imagination. You can make up and tell stories, fairy tales that nobody else can touch. And you can poke fun without being cruel."

Also from Edgewater was Chick Evans, one of the early twentieth century's leading golfers, who eventually retired from the competitive golf circuit in 1967. Evans got his start as an eight-year-old caddy at the Edgewater Golf Club, then located near Broadway and Balmoral. The resultant contacts and experience helped Evans launch his own golf career—and inspired him to eventually set up the Evans Scholars Foundation, which since 1930 has enabled more than eight thousand caddies to go to college. To this day, it remains the country's largest privately funded golf scholarship program.

Among still other local residents who made it big were jazz singer Anita O'Day; author John Jakes, whose string of bestsellers included *North and South* and *The Kent Family Chronicles*; Alan Katz, writer and producer of the *M.A.S.H.* TV series; Harvey Korman, best known for his work on *The Carol Burnett Show*; and comedy writer, director and actor Harold Ramis, whose credits include *Caddyshack*, *National Lampoon's Vacation*, *Ghostbusters*, *Groundhog Day* and *Analyze This.*

"WE SAY NO," PROTESTERS YELLED AT NAVY PLAN TO "MILITARIZE" SENN HIGH SCHOOL

It sounded like a scene from the 1960s even if it was thirty years late. In October 2004, students, parents, teachers and irate community residents packed the auditorium at Senn High School, 5900 North Glenwood, in an effort to shut down plans to turn part of the campus into a Junior Naval ROTC academy. Students gathered at the entrance with signs pleading "Save Senn" in a variety of languages.

Nobody was talking about eliminating the neighborhood school but merely offering the naval program as an option in the same building. The full-time NROTC program would start with about 125 freshmen the following fall and eventually grow to 600 students. "This isn't about recruiting," said

Senn High School under construction, 1913.

David Pickens, an assistant to then school superintendent (and later U.S. education secretary) Arne Duncan.

But the irate students were having none of it. "We need to learn how to read and write, not how to shoot guns," screamed Senn sophomore Emmanuel Banahene.

Army lieutenant colonel Rick Mills, who headed up all the high school–level ROTC programs in the Chicago area, assured everyone the rifles don't actually shoot but are merely used for drills. Students and teachers were not only agitated over the perceived militarization of their school but also worried that the NROTC activities would take over classrooms needed for Senn's 1,719 students.

The program's first speaker, Alderman Mary Ann Smith (48th), began by noting she was the one who brought a tool and die program to Senn and was working to bring in a pre-nursing course. The high school Naval ROTC program had a phenomenal graduation rate (98.1 percent) in the other Chicago public schools where it was already operating. The Senn campus, with a capacity for 2,800 students, had room for over 1,000 more without taking away space from any of the already-existing programs.

Pickens, the next speaker, said he was there to dispel rumors and report facts. He was nearly drowned out by protesters yelling, "We don't want children to die in a war," "No Navy," "Save Senn" and "The military has no place in a high school."

Even Principal Judy Hernandez couldn't control the uproar when Colonel Mills tried to show a video about the program, only to have the protesters chant, "We say no" and stand to turn their backs to the screen.

What followed were more community meetings and a November 29 Chicago Public Schools (CPS) hearing where both the school's supporters and opponents voiced their views.

Two weeks later, two hundred students marched out of the school and headed downtown to protest the Board of Education's approval of the Rickover Naval Academy, named for Hyman Rickover, 1917 CPS graduate who built the U.S. nuclear navy. A handful of students were allowed to speak. Among them was senior class president Yoddite Woldgebrief, who said she had heard from a younger relative that school officials had already been recruiting middle school students for Rickover. "I just feel this whole thing was fixed," she told reporters as she left the meeting in frustration.

CPS officials, with help from U.S. senator Dick Durbin (D-Illinois), helped get a $2.2 million federal grant to open Rickover Academy. Durbin said this would provide another needed option for students and that Senn would be the best site for the Navy ROTC program because it has plenty of space. The school occupies fifteen classrooms, three labs, a gym and eight administrative spaces on two floors on the south wing of the building.

While students across the city can apply, 30 percent of the places are reserved for applicants who live in the area.

Rickover Naval Academy's first graduating class got $3.1 million in scholarships.

Loyola University Just Loves "Living on the Edge"

Ask Jennifer Clark, Loyola University's vice-president for campus and community planning, whether the country's largest Jesuit institution is in Edgewater or Rogers Park. "Both. We're right on the borderline. We like to think we're really 'Living on the Edge,'" she told one local newspaper reporter.

The former St. Ignatius College may have moved from the Near West Side more than a century ago, but it wasn't until 1921 that students and faculty could get off the elevated trains at the Loyola stop. Before that it was the Hayes, named for Hayes Point, a lakefront prairie popular for years as a family picnic area.

In the 1960s, when the neighborhood was starting to get shabby, Loyola gave both Edgewater and Rogers Park a shot in the arm with its "Walk to Work" program, offering housing loans to faculty and staff as a way to encourage them to remain in the community rather than join the flight to the suburbs. From 1977 through the end of 1980, Loyola had arranged for forty-nine mortgage loans totaling $2,500,750. Employees could buy condos or houses in Edgewater or Rogers Park, according to Megs Langdon, a longtime local activist and the program's director. To qualify, faculty and staff had to buy housing within six blocks of Loyola. Each loan was for $8,000 at 6 percent interest. In addition to the mortgage recipients, three hundred Loyola employees were already living within the six-block area. The program tried to encourage its staff not only to be able to walk to work but also to become active members of the area's community organizations, Langdon explained at the time. But it didn't stop there. Loyola's nursing students started helping out at nearby St. Ignatius Church, while other students started getting involved in the area's growing number of homeless shelters.

Perhaps the school's most dramatic event came during Loyola's 1962–63 basketball season, when it took the NCAA championship with a racially integrated team whose coach, George Ireland, had been defying a gentleman's agreement not to play more than three black players at any given time. Since the beginning of the season, Coach Ireland had been putting as many as four black players on the court at one time. In late 1962, Loyola became the first NCAA Division I team to use an all-black lineup, in a game against Wyoming.

Looking south on Sheridan Road in the early 1900s.

Senn High School students dance with fans at an international festival, April 1984. Lerner Newspapers photo.

Classmates at Peirce School, 1910.

Later that season, Loyola trounced an all-white Mississippi State squad, which had itself defied a state order barring it from competing against any school with black players. Because the game obviously couldn't be played in Mississippi, where then-governor Ross Barnett was reportedly ready to have the Mississippi coach arrested to prevent the game from being played, Loyola's Ramblers met the all-white Maroons in Fort Lansing, Michigan, where Loyola won 61–51 and went on to win the NCAA championship.

Mississippi State's president, Dean Colvard, agreed to the match with Loyola, expecting to be fired by Barnett, who had once said there are more blacks living in Mississippi than anywhere else because "they love our way of life here, and that way is segregation."

"It wasn't long before the hate mail started pouring in." Blacks and their supporters were begging, "Please win. This is a great opportunity for the black race," Loyola's captain, Jerry Harkness, recalled on Alabama public radio.

Fifty years later, the Ramblers met the Mississippians, now known as the Bulldogs, once again to mark the anniversary of what some sportswriters call the "Game of Change."

Mundelein/Loyola "Affiliation" Was a Shotgun Wedding as Far as Some Students Were Concerned

Nuns are by nature women of faith, but they were probably never more so than on November 1, 1929—three days after the stock market crash—when they continued as planned with groundbreaking ceremonies for Mundelein College's new Art Deco skyscraper building at 6363 North Sheridan Road.

Despite the grim outlook, class registration began only nineteen months after construction started. In fact, so many students had signed up that the start of classes had to be postponed until October 3, 1930. At the close of Mundelein's first school year, traffic along the Sheridan Road curve was rerouted as bands from Immaculata and St. Mary's High Schools, flanked by Knights of St. Gregory in full regalia, played on the front steps.

Even Pope Pius XI was betting on the 198-foot-tall school. "I don't know if this is the greatest college in the world, but I am sure it's the closest to heaven," the pontiff was quoted in the *Chicago Tribune* the following year. The "Skyscraper College" was part of Cardinal Mundelein's promise to make Catholic education at all levels one of his top priorities.

About a decade after it opened, Mundelein College had twenty-two student societies ranging from an international relations club to a Verse Speaking Choir, which had a contract with NBC radio. Among its members was Golden Globe and Academy Award winner Mercedes McCambridge (class of 1937).

By the late 1950s, forty-eight nuns-in-training were studying alongside Mundelein's regular students, prompting Sister Ann Ida Gannon, Mundelein's longtime president, to set up a theology department. In 1965, she set up a program for women who had dropped out earlier and another for working women who could attend classes on weekends.

During Sister Gannon's regime, the curriculum continued to be expanded beyond the traditional women's college courses to include interior architecture and peace studies. Like most campuses, Mundelein saw its share of political ferment during the 1960s and '70s, at one point hosting farmworkers' union organizer Cesar Chavez and taking part in a nationwide strike protesting the spread of the Vietnam War into Cambodia and the 1970 deaths of four students during an antiwar rally at Kent State University.

In 1980, events marking Mundelein's fiftieth anniversary included the appearance of both Chicago mayor Jane Byrne and Mother Teresa of Calcutta at a golden jubilee dinner where Mother Teresa received the

Cardinal George Mundelein pays a visit to St. Gregory's Church during the 1930s.

university's Magnificat Medal. But by the end of the 1980s, enrollment had plunged and financial resources were drying up, forcing Illinois' last private independent Catholic women's college to tie the knot with Loyola University next door.

But the 985-student school didn't go quietly. After the "affiliation" was announced, some 200 Mundelein women stood in a downpour along Sheridan Road holding drooping signs demanding "Sixty More Years" as they shivered in red and white Mundelein sweatshirts. Some students even vowed to wage a fundraising campaign to bail their alma mater out of the red ink. Asked why, several said they liked being in an all-female environment where they weren't patronizingly referred to as "Mundle Bundles" and they were afraid of being swallowed up by the then 14,000-student Loyola University.

Mundelein was a place for the empowerment of women, who went on to become influential doctors, lawyers, politicians, heads of businesses and educators, as student Meg Ivo said at one of the protest rallies. Nearby, another student was spotted with a sign proclaiming "We don't hate men. We just love our college community."

Vestiges of Mundelein, however, continue in the form of the Gannon Center for Women's Studies and Leadership and the Gannon Scholars Program.

LOCAL ARTIST REMEMBERED FOR ONE OF THE WORLD'S MOST FAMOUS MODERN RELIGIOUS PORTRAITS

Dr. Preston Bradley may have been the voice of liberal Protestantism throughout Uptown and beyond, but many credit Edgewater's now almost forgotten Warner Sallman with literally painting the Face of Christianity. The lifelong North Sider's *Head of Christ* has been reproduced at least 500 million times, easily making the 1940 work the United States' best-known religious painting.

Ironically, many parishioners at Edgewater Covenant Church, 5610 North Glenwood, where he was active until shortly before his 1968 death at Swedish Covenant Hospital, knew him mainly as an usher and Sunday school teacher. Yet while he lived quietly a few blocks away at 5412 North Spaulding, Sallman was already revered as a kind of home-grown Protestant Michelangelo.

Born in 1892, he studied at the Art Institute, worked as a commercial artist in the Loop and, by 1918, was doing illustrations for a variety of religious

This 203-unit Art Deco high-rise at 5040–60 North Marine Drive was built in 1939 as Chicago's first all-electric apartment building. *Photo by the author.*

Clark and Ashland, circa 1920s.

Summerdale Avenue west of Clark Street, circa 1920s.

magazines. He drew for the *Covenant Companion*, which in 1924 published the *Son of Man* charcoal drawing that Sallman said gave the inspiration for his later *Head of Christ*. Over the next fifteen years, *Son of Man* was not only made into prints and rerun twice in the *Companion* but even went on display at the 1933 World's Fair. Sallman also did the artwork for the fair's Salvation Army and American Bible Society exhibits.

The next year, the *Catholic Messenger* put *Son of Man* on a calendar, and in 1935, Sallman was asked to do a special six- by six-foot copy for a revival at North Park College. Members of the North Park Covenant Church reportedly sold neckties to pay for the painting, said to have cost $150 to $200.

Head of Christ was painted over one of Sallman's 1924 prints for the 1940 North Park Seminary Class. Within a year or two, wallet-size reproductions traveled all over the world with American GIs fighting World War II.

During his career, Sallman turned out more than thirty large oils inspired by *Head of Christ*, including *Christ at the Heart's Door* and *Christ Our Pilot*, many of which still hang in churches, hospitals, seminaries and reformatories throughout the country.

Yet he found time to remember August Clausen, his old Sunday school teacher at Lake View Covenant Church, with a painting passed on to Clausen's daughter, Elsie Norman.

His last work, done in 1967, hangs in a church in Rockford. Like the others, it's based on the *Head of Christ*, which has since turned up everywhere from a 750-year-old church on an island off Finland to a Marionite Catholic bookstore in Beirut, Lebanon.

Did Abraham Lincoln Ever Visit Edgewater?

After more than 150 years, local history buffs are still debating whether Abraham Lincoln visited Edgewater.

According to the Edgewater History Association's LeRoy Blommaert, the legend has been going around for years about how the then–presidential candidate met with a group of supporters at Nicholas Kranz's house at 5896 North Ridge, otherwise known as "Seven Mile House" because of its distance from downtown Chicago. Blommaert says the visit is mentioned at least three times—first in a 1936 *Chicago Tribune* story about Peter Kranz's plans to raze the home built by his father in 1849. A second story written

Above: A "Young Lincoln" statue is installed in Senn Park in 1997, recalling the visit some believe the sixteenth president made here during his 1860 campaign.

Left: Edgewater pioneer Nicholas Kranz, who some say played host to Lincoln.

The Kranz family home at Clark Street and Ridge Avenue, once known as the "Seven Mile House" because of its distance from downtown Chicago. Speculation still simmers over whether Abraham Lincoln met there with local residents during the 1860 presidential campaign.

by John Drury in the *Chicago Daily News* quotes Kranz telling about how "Lincoln was brought to my father's place to attend a Republican caucus of farmers in the vicinity…My father was a Republican and an admirer of Lincoln." And in an August 3, 1986 *Chicago Tribune* article, Abigail Foerster recalled how "from the porch of the Seven Mile House, an inn operated by Nicholas Kranz on a homestead where Senn High School now stands, presidential candidate Abraham Lincoln addressed a Republican caucus of farmers." A statue of a young Lincoln on the site of the Kranz homestead gives the story further credence, Blommaert conceded.

But not so fast, says Blommaert. In a 1989 interview with Gloria Evenson for the Edgewater Historical Society's oral history project, Lois Kranz, Peter's granddaughter, recalls hearing her grandfather talk about Lincoln's visit numerous times. And while she believed Lincoln probably did visit Seven Mile House, she admitted her grandfather loved to tell stories and "was known to exaggerate and his stories became embellished with time."

While "the story is possible" and "we'd all like to believe it's true" and that getting to the Seven Mile House would not have been difficult, for Lincoln, Blommaert remains skeptical. Because "Lincoln is one of the most studied and written about men who ever lived...a compilation has been made of all his actions and whereabouts almost day to day," and "this compilation shows he visited Chicago on only two occasions in 1860," neither of them while he was a presidential candidate. Blommaert added that the only source for the story was Peter Kranz. Wouldn't someone else have talked or written about the visit over the years? Peter Kranz was only about two years old when Lincoln supposedly came to visit, Blommaert noted. If Peter Kranz was told about it later, why didn't anyone else seem to remember?

So while it's certain Lincoln passed through Edgewater at least five times on the train, "passed through doesn't have the cachet of a visit. But we know for sure at least that happened," Bloomaert said.

And much as everyone might like to believe Lincoln visited here, he added, he probably didn't.

What's in a Street Name? Sometimes a Lot More Here Than What You Might Think

Why was Sulzer Road—named for Lake View township's first white settler—renamed Montrose Avenue (4400 North) in honor of a little-remembered (by Americans at least) Scottish general who fought alongside England's King Charles I against Oliver Cromwell? You'd have to ask the city fathers who changed it back in the mid-nineteenth century. But street changes were pretty commonplace back then.

Broadway (600 West at 2800 North to 1200 West at 6358 North) started out as Evanston Avenue, apparently because that's where it eventually led. It was renamed in honor of the famous New York thoroughfare at the behest of local merchants who had also had their community christened Uptown to promote an image of sophisticated affluence back when the neighborhood was becoming Chicago's answer to Manhattan's Great White Way, which was itself once known to Indians and early colonists as the Wickquasgek Trail. Why the name was changed remains unclear, but then many if not most Uptown/Edgewater street names honor either obscure historical figures or little-remembered developers.

Clark Street, named for Revolutionary War hero George Rogers Clark, who captured the Northwest Territory (which included present-day Chicago) from the British, was originally known as Green Bay Road because it went all the way to Green Bay, Wisconsin.

Clarendon Avenue (800 West from 3928 to 4746 North) honors Edward Hyde, earl of Clarendon, who served England's King Charles in exile and after the monarchy's restoration. Windsor Street (4532 West) tips the hat to Windsor Castle and the House of Windsor, the family name adopted by Great Britain's Hanover royal family during World War I. On the other hand, Castlewood Terrace has nothing to do with anyone's castle but, rather, 1890s developer Charles Castle.

Catalpa Avenue (5500 North) is named for a street of the same name in Edgewater founder John L. Cochran's Philadelphia hometown. Cochran named Glenlake Avenue for Glen Lake, New York. He also named Devon (6400 North), Ardmore (5800 North), Bryn Mawr (5600 North), Rosemont (6300 North), Wayne (1332 West) and Berwyn (5300 North) for some of the stops along the Philadelphia Main Line commuter route. And having been born in Sacramento, California, before his family moved east, Cochran is believed to have named Hollywood Avenue (5700 North) for the Los Angeles suburb sometimes called Tinseltown. Cochran probably named Granville (6200 North) for Granville, New York, although according to *Streetwise Chicago* authors Don Hayner and Tom McNamee, some claim the street could have been named for another developer, Granville Bates, or even for one of Chicago's earliest schoolteachers, Granville Sproat. And again, no surprise—Cochran named Edgewater Avenue (5732 North) for his own development.

But Cochran wasn't the only developer to leave names on Edgewater and Uptown lamp posts. Hood Avenue (6150 North) is either named for Robert Hood, a land developer in the early 1870s, or David Hood, a local landowner who lived on Ridge Avenue in 1847.

Gunnison Street (4832 North) was probably named for developer Frederick Gunnison and runs through part of his firm's subdivision. Another theory is that it honors U.S. Army captain John Gunnison, a soldier/explorer who made an 1841 survey of the area around Lake Michigan. He was later murdered and his body mutilated by Indians in Utah.

Considering so many early Chicagoans hailed from back east, it isn't surprising that Clifton Avenue (1226 West from 1900 to 4700 North) is named for a town in New Jersey. Dover Street (1400 West from 4400 to 4756 North) is named for the capital of Delaware. Buena Avenue (4200 North) was possibly named for a New Jersey borough by Edward Waller, a real estate developer from that state.

The namers of still other streets had to go a little farther than the eastern seaboard for ideas. Elmdale (6000 North) is named for the city of Elmadalen,

Sweden, while Highland Avenue (6330 North) was probably named for Highland Park, a North Shore suburb.

Foster Avenue (5200 North) was named for Dr. John H. Foster, who served as a surgeon in the Black Hawk War and ended up in Chicago only to settle the affairs of his dead brother, an army officer who was murdered while trying to discipline a drunken soldier. Dr. Foster decided to stay permanently and eventually became a member of both the Chicago and Illinois Boards of Education. He died at age seventy-eight when he was thrown from his carriage and landed headfirst on Division Street.

Again, no surprise: a number of streets were named for the developers who carved out the subdivisions those streets ran through. L.B. Giddings, a prominent land investor in the mid-nineteenth century, for example, gave his name to Giddings Street (4732 North running from 2000 to 6356 West). And of course, Warner Avenue (4132 North) is named for L.A. Warner, another leading North Side developer back in the 1870s. Cuyler Avenue (4032 North) remembers Edward J. Cuyler, who migrated to Chicago from Essex County, New York, as a Chicago & North Western Railroad paymaster who stayed with that job until the tracks were laid as far north as Janesville, Wisconsin. Gordon Terrace (4182 North from 632 to 948 West) was named for G.H. Gordon, another real estate subdivider, while Grace Street (3800 North) was named for Grace Gurnee, the daughter of developer Walter Gurnee, who also happened to be Chicago's mayor in the early 1850s. Leavitt Street (2200 West) is named for David Leavitt, a New York banker and Illinois and Michigan Canal trustee in the 1840s.

Other streets were named by promoters for an area's natural beauty. Eastwood Avenue (4632 North) was named by the Northwest Land Association for a pine forest in the Ravenswood Gardens area. Glenwood Avenue (1400 West from 4900 to 7600 North) ran through a wooded area that at the time had a number of narrow valleys or glens.

Others, of course, were named for long-forgotten politicians. Cullom Avenue (4300 North) honors Shelby Moore Cullom, who served fifty-two years in one elected office or another, a record he reminded anyone who would listen that "exceeded in length of unbroken service that of any other public man in the country's history." That national service marathon included six years in Congress, a decade in the Illinois General Assembly, six years as Illinois governor and thirty years as a U.S. senator. While in the Senate, Cullom shepherded passage of the Interstate Commerce Act and was appointed by President William McKinley to oversee creation of a Hawaiian territorial government after the islands' kingdom was overthrown.

In addition to a street in Chicago, the village of Cullom, Illinois, is named in his honor.

Also honored with a street (at 1434 West from 2200 to 4924 North) was Alderman Bernard Janssen, who represented a constituency southwest of North Avenue and the lake for only one term (from 1877 to 1879). Nobody remembers what he ever did as an alderman.

Still other streets like Irving Park Road (4000 North) are named for literary figures like Washington Irving, author of *The Legend of Sleepy Hollow*, among other classics. The one-time Indian portage trail linking Lake Michigan with the Des Plaines River spawned a small settlement named Irvington, which later became today's Old Irving Park, a solidly established suburb by the mid-1870s.

Kenmore Avenue (1038 West) was named after the Fredericksburg, Virginia home of Colonel Fielding Lewis, whose wife, Betty, was General George Washington's sister. Talk about reaching for straws!

Despite what you'd think, Magnolia Avenue (1232 West) isn't named for a flower but a tugboat whose skipper, Joseph Gilson, has been all but forgotten despite his heroism during the 1871 Chicago Fire. According to a pamphlet making the rounds just after the fire, Gilson was getting ready to load all his family's belongings on the *Magnolia* when he spotted burning ships and trapped people along the waterfront. Before coming to their rescue, Gilson reportedly lassoed a burning boat and pulled it away from a pier full of stranded people. That done, he turned back and hauled crowded boats farther out into the lake, away from the heat and flames. The anonymous pamphlet noted that Gilson's boat was the last to leave the river.

Some street names are more obvious. Farragut Avenue (5232 North) was of course named for Civil War hero David Glasgow Farragut, the U.S. Navy's first admiral. And Olive Avenue (5632 North) celebrates just what it says it does: the olive tree.

On the other hand, if you thought Wilson Avenue (4600 North) was named for our twenty-eighth president, you'd be wrong. The one-time Uptown "Main Street" is named after John P. Wilson, a lawyer who wrote the laws creating the Chicago Metropolitan Sanitary District (now the Chicago Water Reclamation District). But it was Wilson's sheer willpower, so to speak, that probably helped ensure a future for Children's Memorial Hospital (CMH). According to *Streetwise Chicago*, Wilson set aside $330,000 for the hospital, provided the hospital could raise twice that on its own. If not, CMH would only have gotten $50,000, with the rest of the money to be divided among Wilson's three children. One of his daughters who was on the hospital's board set to work trying to raise the money. She found someone willing to donate half the money needed, putting the fundraising drive over the top with the help of the other Wilson children. It was a remarkable example of self-sacrifice on the part of the Wilsons. For had the hospital failed to raise the $660,000, each of the three Wilson heirs would have been more than $100,000 richer.

Bibliography

Asbury, Herbert. *Gem of the Prairie.* New York: Alfred A. Knopf, 1940.

Bernstein, Arnie. *Hollywood on Lake Michigan.* Chicago: Lake Claremont Press, 1998.

Edgewater Historical Association archives, Chicago.

Encyclopedia of Chicago. Developed by the Newberry Library with the cooperation of the Chicago Historical Society. Chicago: Newberry Library, 2004.

Grossman, Ron. *Guide to Chicago Neighborhoods.* Chicago: New Century Publishers, 1981.

Hayner, Don, and Tom McNamee. *Streetwise Chicago.* Chicago: Loyola University Press, 1988.

Heise, Kenan, and Mark Frazel. *Hands on Chicago.* Chicago: Bonus Books, 1987.

Houlihan, Mike. *Hooliganism Stories.* Chicago: Dog Ear Publishing, 2008.

Keating, Ann Durkin. *Chicago Neighborhoods and Suburbs: An Historical Guide.* Chicago: Bonus Books, 2008.

Lerner Newspapers. Chicago, 1965–1993.

Lindberg, Richard. *Return Again to the Scene of the Crime.* Nashville, TN: Cumberland House, 2001.

———. *Return to the Scene of the Crime.* Nashville, TN: Cumberland House, 1999.

———. *To Serve and Collect.* Westport, CT: Praeger, 1991.
Lydon, Jacki. *Legends and Landmarks of Uptown.* Chicago: Jacki Lydon, 1970.
Miller, Donald L. *City of the Century.* Chicago: Simon & Schuster, 2003.
Pacyga, Dominic A. *Chicago.* Chicago: University of Chicago Press, 2003.

About the Author

Patrick Butler is a lifelong Chicagoan who has covered the North Side for the past forty-five years, most of them as a reporter for the Lerner Newspapers. He currently writes for Inside Publications' *Booster* and *News-Star*. Butler has served more than a dozen years as president of the Ravenswood–Lake View Historical Association and for several years anchored a cable TV news/feature magazine, *North Side Neighbors*.

Visit us at
www.historypress.net

This title is also available as an e-book

www.ingramcontent.com/pod-product-compliance
Lightning Source LLC
LaVergne TN
LVHW052342100826
845147LV00021B/1152

* 9 7 8 1 6 2 6 1 9 1 4 3 3 *